The
Ancient
Egyptian
Books of
the Afterlife

The Ancient Egyptian Books of the Afterlife

ERIK HORNUNG

Translated from the German by David Lorton

CORNELL UNIVERSITY PRESS

ITHACA AND LONDON

First published 1999 by Cornell University Press
First printing, Cornell Paperbacks, 1999

Printed in the United States of America

Hornung, Erik.
    [Altägyptische Jenseitsbücher. English]
    The ancient Egyptian books of the afterlife / Eric Hornung :
translated from the German by David Lorton.
        p.   cm.
    Includes bibliographical references and index.
    ISBN 0-8014-3515-3 (cloth : alk. paper).—ISBN 0-8014-8515-0
(paper : alk. paper)
    1. Incantations, Egyptian.   2. Future life.   3. Egypt—Religion.
I. Title.
PJ1551.H67   1999
299'.31—dc21   99-10888
                                                              CIP

Cornell University Press strives to use environmentally responsible suppliers and materials to the fullest extent possible in the publishing of its books. Such materials include vegetable-based, low-VOC inks and acid-free papers that are recycled, totally chlorine-free, or partly composed of nonwood fibers.

Cloth printing
10 9 8 7 6 5 4 3 2 1

Paperback printing
10 9 8 7 6 5 4 3 2 1

Dedicated to the memory of
Friedrich Abitz (1924–1994) and
Abdel-Aziz Fahmy Sadek (1933–1995)

CONTENTS

TRANSLATOR'S NOTE

No single set of conventions exists for the English rendering of ancient Egyptian and modern Arabic personal and place names. Most of the names mentioned in this book occur in a standard reference work: John Baines and Jaromír Málek, *Atlas of Ancient Egypt* (New York: Facts on File, 1980), and the renderings here follow that volume. The only exception is the omission of the typographical sign for *ayin;* this consonant does not exist in English, and I felt that its inclusion would serve only as a distraction.

Erik Hornung's summary of the Books of the Afterlife provides a much-needed synopsis of this material for both scholars and general readers, and I thank Cornell University Press for asking me to participate in this project. I also thank Professor Hornung and Eckhard Eichler for their help and encouragement while it was under way.

D. L.

ABBREVIATIONS

BD   Book of the Dead
BM   British Museum
Cat.   Catalogo (of the Turin Museum)
CG   Catalogue général (of the Cairo Museum)
KV   Valley of the Kings (or King's Valley)
MMA   Metropolitan Museum of Art
P.   Papyrus
QV   Valley of the Queens (or Queen's Valley)
TT   Theban tomb

Abbreviations of titles of journals and monograph series are found in the bibliography at the end of this volume.

ENGLISH TRANSLATIONS

Nearly all the compositions discussed here have been translated into English. The bibliography at the end of this volume will be consulted primarily by Egyptologists; a list of relatively accessible translations, in order of publication, is supplied here for the convenience of nonspecialists. While I include some older sources here because of their availability in reprint editions, readers should note that because of ongoing advances in our knowledge and understandings, relatively recent sources are generally more reliable than older ones.

D. L.

The Pyramid Texts

Samuel A. B. Mercer, *The Pyramid Texts in Translation and Commentary*, 4 vols. (New York, 1942).

John A. Wilson, in James B. Pritchard, ed., *Ancient Near Eastern Texts Relating to the Old Testament*, 2d ed. (Princeton, 1955), pp. 3, 32–33 (selections).

Raymond O. Faulkner, *The Ancient Egyptian Pyramid Texts*, 2 vols. (Oxford, 1969).

——, in Raymond O. Faulkner, Edward F. Wente, Jr., and William Kelly Simpson, *The Literature of Ancient Egypt: An Anthology of Stories, Instructions, and Poetry* (New Haven, 1972), pp. 269–278 (selections).

Miriam Lichtheim, *Ancient Egyptian Literature: A Book of Readings*, vol. 1: *The Old and Middle Kingdoms* (Berkeley, 1973), pp. 29–50 (selections).

Marshall Clagett, *Ancient Egyptian Science: A Source Book*, vol. 1 (Philadelphia, 1989), pp. 413–424 (selections).

The Coffin Texts

John A. Wilson, in James B. Pritchard, ed., *Ancient Near Eastern Texts Related to the Old Testament*, 2d ed. (Princeton, 1955), pp. 7–8, 10, 11–12, 33 (selections).

Leonard H. Lesko, *The Ancient Egyptian Book of the Two Ways*, UCBUCP 17 (Berkeley, 1972).

Miriam Lichtheim, *Ancient Egyptian Literature: A Book of Readings*, vol. 1: *The Old and Middle Kingdoms* (Berkeley, 1973), pp. 131–133 (selections).

Alexandre Piankoff, *The Wandering of the Soul*, Bollingen Series 40/6 (New York, 1974) ("Book of the Two Ways").

Raymond O. Faulkner, *The Ancient Egyptian Coffin Texts*, 3 vols. (Warminster, 1973–1978; rpt. 1994).

Marshall Clagett, *Ancient Egyptian Science: A Source Book*, vol. 1 (Philadelphia, 1989), pp. 437–443 (selections).

The Book of the Dead

John A. Wilson, in James B. Pritchard, ed., *Ancient Near Eastern Texts Related to the Old Testament*, 2d ed. (Princeton, 1955), pp. 3–4, 9–10, 34–36 (selections).

Miriam Lichtheim, *Ancient Egyptian Literature: A Book of Readings*, vol. 2: *The New Kingdom* (Berkeley, 1976), pp. 119–132 (selections).

Raymond O. Faulkner, *The Ancient Egyptian Book of the Dead*, ed. Carol Andrews (London, 1985).

Eva von Dassow, ed., *The Egyptian Book of the Dead: The Book of Going Forth by Day* (San Francisco, 1994).

The Amduat

E. A. Wallis Budge, *The Egyptian Heaven and Hell* (London, 1905), vols. 1 (long version) and 2, pp. 1–40 (short version).

Alexandre Piankoff, *The Tomb of Ramesses VI*, Bollingen Series 40/1 (New York, 1954).

——, *The Shrines of Tut-Ankh-Amon*, Bollingen Series 40/2 (New York, 1955; rpt. 1962), pp. 79–83, 85–89 (selections).

Marshall Clagett, *Ancient Egyptian Science: A Source Book*, vol. 1 (Philadelphia, 1989), pp. 491–506 (introductions to the individual hours).

The Spell of the Twelve Caves

Alexandre Piankoff, *The Wandering of the Soul*, Bollingen Series 40/6 (Princeton, 1974), pp. 40–114 (see also above on "The Book of the Dead"; this composition is spell 168).

The Book of Gates

E. A. Wallis Budge, *The Egyptian Heaven and Hell*, vol. 2 (London, 1905), pp. 43–306.

Alexandre Piankoff, *The Tomb of Ramesses VI*, Bollingen Series 40/1 (New York, 1954), pp. 137–224.

The Enigmatic Book of the Netherworld

Alexandre Piankoff, *The Shrines of Tut-Ankh-Amon*, Bollingen Series 40/2 (New York, 1955; rpt. 1962), pp. 121–125, 127–131.

The Book of Caverns

Alexandre Piankoff, *The Tomb of Ramesses VI*, Bollingen Series 40/1 (New York, 1954), pp. 45–135.

The Book of the Earth

Alexandre Piankoff, *The Tomb of Ramesses VI*, Bollingen Series 40/1 (New York, 1954), pp. 327–376.

The Book of Nut

James P. Allen, *Genesis in Egypt: The Philosophy of Ancient Egyptian Creation Accounts*, YES 2 (New Haven, 1988), pp. 1–7.
Marshall Clagett, *Ancient Egyptian Science: A Source Book*, vol. 2 (Philadelphia, 1995), pp. 357–403.

The Book of the Day

Alexandre Piankoff, *The Tomb of Ramesses VI*, Bollingen Series 40/1 (New York, 1954), pp. 389–407.

The Book of the Night

Alexandre Piankoff, *The Tomb of Ramesses VI*, Bollingen Series 40/1 (New York, 1954), pp. 409–428.

The Litany of Re

Alexandre Piankoff, *The Litany of Re*, Bollingen Series 40/4 (New York, 1964).
Marshall Clagett, *Ancient Egyptian Science: A Source Book*, vol. 1 (Philadelphia, 1989), pp. 511–529.

The Book of the Heavenly Cow

John A. Wilson, in James B. Pritchard, ed., *Ancient Near Eastern Texts Relating to the Old Testament*, 2d ed. (Princeton, 1955), pp. 8–9, 10–11 (partial).
R. T. Rundle Clark, *Myth and Symbol in Ancient Egypt* (London, 1959), pp. 181–185 (partial).

Alexandre Piankoff, *The Shrines of Tut-Ankh-Amon*, Bollingen Series 40/2 (New York, 1955; rpt. 1962), pp. 26–37.

Miriam Lichtheim, *Ancient Egyptian Literature: A Book of Readings*, vol. 2: *The New Kingdom* (Berkeley, 1976), pp. 197–199 (partial).

Marshall Clagett, *Ancient Egyptian Science: A Source Book*, vol. 1 (Philadelphia, 1989), pp. 537–542 (partial).

PREFACE

Early Egyptologists focused primarily on the collection of spells that Lepsius designated the Book of the Dead, which is often viewed as the "Bible of the ancient Egyptians." With the discovery of the Pyramid Texts in 1880–1881, research interest turned to that collection of spells, which is nearly a thousand years earlier. The Book of the Dead, however, still remains at the center of all esoteric interest in ancient Egypt.

But the other large group of texts dealing with the afterlife, the Books of the Netherworld (once also called Guides to the Afterlife) long led a shadowy existence. Their actual discoverer was Jean-François Champollion, who saw these compositions when he visited the Valley of the Kings in 1829 and immediately recognized their significance. In the thirteenth of his letters from Egypt, dated May 26, 1829, he gives a detailed account of the decoration of the royal tombs accessible in his day, especially that of the tomb of Ramesses VI, where he completed a number of copies and descriptions. He had prepared the first translation from the Book of Gates and the Book of Caverns when his untimely death cut short his work. Later in the nineteenth century, Gaston Maspero and Eugène Lefébure in particular devoted themselves to deciphering the Books of the Afterlife. In time, however, a widespread, rather negative attitude emerged toward these "abstruse" priestly fantasies, as they were adjudged, and leading specialists no longer deemed it worthwhile to become involved with them.

It is typical that the discovery of the tomb of Tutankhamun in 1922 aroused the world's interest in the material riches of the Valley of the Kings while creating no momentum for the study of its spiritual treasures. In the mid-1930s, Alexandre Piankoff (1897–1966) was the first to undertake a systematic study of the religious books in the royal tombs, and he issued a steady stream of text editions, translations, and other works. With his splendid edition of the tomb of Ramesses VI in 1954, which was prepared under the auspices of the Bollingen Foundation, he made practically all the relevant texts available in English translation. Further study of the royal Books of the Afterlife could now be built on these foundations.

Beginning in 1958, I had the pleasure of working with Piankoff, after Siegfried Schott had repeatedly called my attention to the Books of the Netherworld. Meanwhile, they have been generally recognized as an important source for the history of Egyptian religion, and especially for beliefs regarding the afterlife, and they have even received attention outside the field of Egyptology, especially from members of the Jungian school of psychoanalysis.

The Books of the Netherworld are the focus of this book; I shall treat such "classical" sources as the Pyramid Texts, the Coffin Texts, and the Book of the Dead more summarily, since other aids to understanding them are already available. Additionally, in all periods the Egyptian mortuary cult employed numerous other texts, which have been designated "mortuary liturgies" (in German, *Verklärungen*), to which Jan Assmann has devoted special attention.

It is an open question to what extent these compositions, which are so distinct in form, reflect a monolithic conception of the afterlife. The New Kingdom undoubtedly added fresh accents of its own: we can characterize the difference between the Book of the Dead and the Books of the Netherworld by noting that only the latter actually give detailed *descriptions* of the hereafter; the spells of the Book of the Dead are concerned with practical assistance regarding the journey to the afterlife and the deceased's stay there. There was also an effort to maintain a hierarchy of compositions, so that some of them—the Pyramid Texts, the Books of the Netherworld, and the Books of the Sky—were reserved for the exclusive use of Pharaoh, just as certain forms of architecture and measurement served only for use in the realm of royalty.

Most of the books and collections of spells treated here were still in use in the Late Period. At that time, whole libraries of ancient writings were collected on tomb walls and sarcophagi for use in the afterlife, though there was a preference for liturgical texts handed down in the cult. All the conditions were thus at hand for an influence that continued beyond the pharaonic period and into the new spiritual currents of Hellenism and early Christianity. In the Books of the Netherworld, as in classical esoterica, the "sun at midnight" stood at the center of the experience of the afterlife, and along with the myth of Osiris the course of the sun played an important role in the Hellenistic Isis mysteries. The disclosure of such relationships represents a wide field for investigation, though historians of religion are too little familiar with these texts.

On the whole, however, research into the texts and representations has yielded rich results in recent years, so that it seems time to venture a summary and orientation for nonspecialists, who are otherwise confronted by a growing body of literature. To facilitate the survey, I have added drawings of the individual nocturnal hours or sections of the Books of the Netherworld and the Sky. I thank Dr. Abdel Ghaffer Shedid for his kind permission to employ his views of the Books of the Netherworld from the *Komparative Untersuchungen zu vier Unterwelts-büchern* of Winfried Barta (see figures 1–12, 14–25, 28–36, and 38) and Dr. Gilles Roulin for the preparation of additional figures.

CHRONOLOGY

Archaic Period   c. 3000–2700 B.C.E.

  Dynasties 1 and 2

Old Kingdom   c. 2705–2180 B.C.E.

  Dynasty 3 (Djoser); first pyramids   2705–2640 B.C.E.
  Dynasty 4 (Khufu, Khephren)   2640–2520 B.C.E.
  Dynasty 5 (Wenis); first Pyramid Texts   2520–2360 B.C.E.
  Dynasty 6 (Teti, Pepy I, Pepy II)   2360–2195 B.C.E.
  Dynasty 8 (Ibi)   2195–2180 B.C.E.

First Intermediate Period   c. 2180–1987 B.C.E.

  Dynasties 9–10; capital at Herakleopolis
  Dynasty 11; capital at Thebes; contemporaneous
    with Dynasties 9–10

Middle Kingdom (Coffin Texts)   c. 1987–1640 B.C.E.

  Dynasty 11 (Mentuhotpe)   1987–1938 B.C.E.
  Dynasty 12 (Amenemhet, Senwosret)   1938–1759 B.C.E.
  Dynasties 13–14   1759–1640 B.C.E.

Second Intermediate Period   c. 1640–1530 B.C.E.

Dynasties 15–16 (Hyksos rulers)
Dynasty 17; capital at Thebes; contemporaneous
   with Dynasties 15–16

New Kingdom (Book of the Dead)   c. 1540–1075 B.C.E.

Dynasty 18; Amduat, Litany of Re, Book
   of Gates, etc.   1540–1292 B.C.E.
Dynasty 19 (Ramesside rulers); Book of Caverns,
   Books of the Sky   1292–1190 B.C.E.
Dynasty 20 (Ramesside rulers); Book of the Earth   1190–1075 B.C.E.

Third Intermediate Period   c. 1075–664 B.C.E.

Dynasty 21; flowering of painted sarcophagi
   and papyri at Thebes   1075–945 B.C.E.
Dynasties 22–24 (Libyan rulers)   945–712 B.C.E.
Dynasty 25 ("Ethiopian" rulers)   740–664 B.C.E.

Late Period   664–332 B.C.E.

Dynasty 26 ("Saite" rulers)   664–525 B.C.E.
Dynasty 27 (Persian rulers)   525–404 B.C.E.
Dynasties 28–30 (last native rulers)   404–342 B.C.E.

Macedonians   332–305 B.C.E.

Ptolemaic Period   305–30 B.C.E.

Roman and Byzantine Periods   30 B.C.E.-642 C.E.

The
Ancient
Egyptian
Books of
the Afterlife

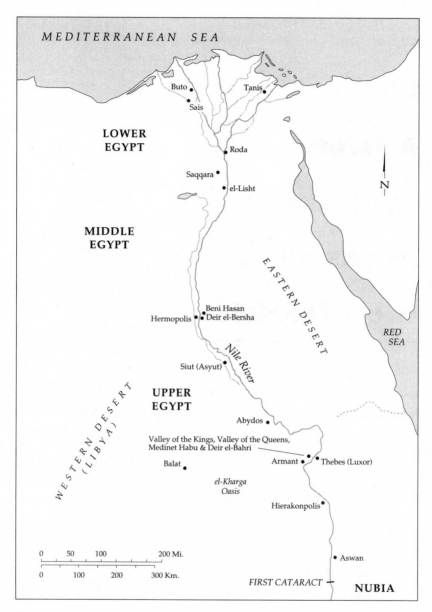

Egypt

THE PYRAMID TEXTS

Sources

The Pyramid Texts represent the oldest collection of religious spells preserved from ancient Egypt. Beginning with Wenis, the last king of Dynasty 5 (c. 2350 B.C.E.), varying selections of spells were carved in all the royal pyramids of the Old Kingdom, especially in the sarcophagus chambers and their antechambers. In the case of Teti, they also appeared on the royal sarcophagus, and with Pepy I, the inscriptions began to extend beyond the antechamber (figures 1 and 2). After 2200 B.C.E., under Pepy II, they were also employed in the pyramids of queens, and after the end of the Old Kingdom, they appeared on the tomb walls and coffins of officials. In the Middle Kingdom, the pyramids were free of texts, so that when Wenis's version appeared in the mastaba of Senwosretankh at Lisht, it was practically unaltered; many pyramid spells, however, continued to be employed on coffins of this period. In the New Kingdom, they occurred in the tombs of some officials and on royal sarcophagi. Spells from this corpus were still in use in the Late Period, in tombs and on sarcophagi.

In the Old Kingdom, spells were included in the pyramids of kings Wenis, Teti, Pepy I, Merenre I, Pepy II, and Ibi and those of queens Wedjebten, Neith, and Iput. In the pyramids of the queens and that of Ibi, the spells were concentrated in a single room; the earlier pyramids also included them in the antechamber and the end of the subterranean corridor.

1. Hieroglyphs from the Pyramid Texts of the pyramid of Wenis. Photo copyright © Al Berens, Suredesign Graphics.

Research

The spells were discovered when Gaston Maspero opened the pyramids, work he began in 1880 and concluded in May 1881 with the opening of the pyramid of Teti. As early as 1882, Maspero began an edition and translation of the texts, starting with those from the pyramid of Wenis, and his ongoing articles in the *Receuil de travaux* also appeared in book form in 1894. In 1899, Kurt Sethe took up the Pyramid Texts for inclusion in the *Wörterbuch der ägytischen Sprache* (Dictionary of the Egyptian Language), and in 1908 he produced a text edition that still remains definitive. The textual basis was substantially expanded by the investigations of Gustave Jéquier in southern Saqqara from 1924 to 1936, in the course of which he was able to secure considerably more spells in the pyramid of Pepy II while also discovering the versions in the pyramids of queens Wedjebten (1925–1926), Neith, and Iput (1931–1932) and in the later tomb of Ibi. In March 1951, Jean-Philippe Lauer and Jean

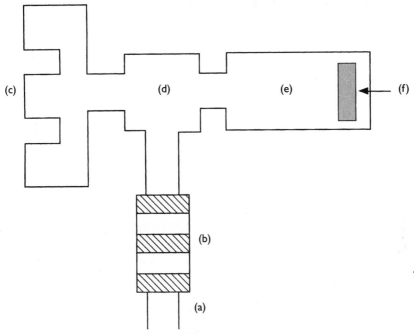

2. The subterranean portion of the pyramid of Wenis: (a) entrance corridor, (b) three portcullises, (c) three statue niches, (d) antechamber, (e) sarcophagus chamber, (f) sarcophagus. Adapted from Kurt Sethe, *Die altägyptischen Pyramidentexte*, vol. 3 (Leipzig, 1922), p. 116. Drawing by David Lorton.

Sainte-Fare Garnot launched a systematic investigation of the pyramids of Dynasty 6; after a rather long interruption, Lauer continued the work with Jean Leclant, and they discovered many additional fragments in the pyramids of Teti (more than 700), Pepy I (more than 2,000), and Merenre.

After Maspero's provisional translation, a further rendering by Louis Speleers, which relied on the preparatory work of Sethe, appeared in French in 1924; the full English translation by Samuel A. B. Mercer that appeared in 1952 has since been superseded by that of Raymond O. Faulkner in 1969. The translation and extensive commentary prepared and continually revised by Sethe was not published until after his death. The volumes appeared from 1935 to 1962, with publication interrupted by World War II.

Investigation of questions of detail began in 1914 with Pierre Lacau's comprehensive work on the suppression and mutilation of signs and continued with G. van der Leeuw's 1916 work on conceptions of the divine. James Henry Breasted drew on the Pyramid Texts for his influential *Development of Religion and Thought in Ancient Egypt,* which appeared in 1912. In the early days of research, the texts were dated as early as possible; Sethe assumed that the majority of them stemmed from predynastic times. The result was a belief that with these spells, one could trace the very beginnings of Egyptian culture and religion. Today, however, scholars are inclined to date the texts' origin as close as possible to the time they were recorded, though we still lack individual studies devoted to dating them more exactly.

Structure and Language

The texts, which differ considerably in length and were not illustrated, were carved in vertical columns on the walls of the pyramids' subterranean spaces. The outlines of the signs were painted green, indicating the hoped-for regeneration of the deceased. With the exception of spell 355 ("Opening the Double Door of the Sky"), the spells lack titles, with the result that in Dynasty 6, every column begins with the notation "words to be spoken," a phrase that appears only at the beginnings of spells in the pyramid of Wenis. The ends of the spells are marked by a horizontal line in the case of Wenis and by a hieroglyph for "house" in the later pyramids. In his edition Sethe distinguished 714 spells; Faulkner increased the number to 759 in 1969, though some of these spells are duplicates and should not have been included. Some of the spells were originally composed in the first person singular for the royal burial ritual but were transposed into the third person when they were recorded in the pyramids.

The order in which the spells are to be read remains unclear. Maspero and Sethe began with the north wall of the sarcophagus chamber, whereas Siegfried Schott and Alexandre Piankoff regarded their inception as lying at the entrance to the antechamber. Schott, Hartwig Altenmüller, and Joachim Spiegel have attempted to explain the sequence of spells as the royal burial ritual; Schott and Altenmüller included the royal mortuary temple in the ritual performance, whereas Spiegel (who, like Altenmüller, confined his study to the pyramid of Wenis) set all its events in the less spacious confines of the pyramid's interior. Jürgen Osing, employing the example of Wenis, has pointed to a thematic division—for example, apotropaic spells at the entrance and offering texts in the sarcophagus chamber—that speaks against the continuous text of a ritual, as do the dramatic changes and differing division of the content from pyramid to pyramid. Nevertheless, it is scarcely to be denied that these are overwhelmingly ritual texts. On the analogy of the later corpora, we can suppose that the texts were selected from a larger collection for very distinct purposes and arranged according to distinctive points of view. There is no recognizable orientation to the four cardinal points.

The language of the texts is Old Egyptian, though in a relatively antiquated form displaying some phonological and grammatical differences from the other texts of the Old Kingdom; the orthography was still in the process of development and employed highly redundant writings. This was the earliest use of retrograde writing, that is, the reversal of the normal sequence of the columns. The avoidance of complete figures of animals and people is striking, as is their deliberate mutilation. The fear that such signs might spring to life and pose a danger played a role here, along with, probably, the desire to protect the offerings of the deceased king from other living beings.

Content

According to Sethe's count, the pyramid of Wenis contains 227 spells; fresh spells were included in each of the subsequent pyramids, though we still lack studies regarding changes in content and shifts in thematic emphasis. Generally speaking, the texts were supposed to be of special service to the deceased king in his ascent to the sky and his reception in the divine realm. In this regard, every suitable means of assistance was included: a ladder or ramp leading up to the sky, clouds, storms, hail, incense, sunlight, and animal forms such as a bird, a beetle, or a locust. The god Shu, who held up the sky, was an especially suitable helper. Moreover, the spells communicate knowledge to Pharaoh regarding the ways and places in the hereafter, as well as dangers he could encounter there. Dialogues with guardians of gateways and with a ferryman supply specific knowledge that would enable the deceased king to name the correct names and answer all questions correctly in order to prove his legitimacy and make his way through the regions of the hereafter.

The topography of the hereafter remains somewhat indeterminate, though the Field of Reeds, the Field of Offerings, the Lake of the Jackal, and the Winding Waterway receive emphasis as important locales. The sky was evidently traversed by water so that deities and deceased crossed it by boat, and the dead were dependent on the services of the ferryman. The Duat does not yet seem to have been fixed in the nether-world but rather appears to have included celestial regions. Neverthe-less, it was not a desirable place to stay, and even the sun god Re was portrayed as being there "in fetters" from which only sunrise could free him (spell 254, § 285). The violent arrival of the king in the sky is de-picted in an especially striking manner in the Cannibal Hymn of spells 273–274. Because the king is repeatedly identified with the creator god Atum, we encounter many allusions to this deity's act of creation.

The provisioning of the deceased, their freedom of movement, and the repelling of inimical beings also play prominent roles; the ritual "smashing of the red pots" (spell 244) aims at the annihilation of all ene-mies. A considerable number of magical spells directed against serpents (and also scorpions: 227) shows that spells from this life were trans-posed to the afterlife to deal with similar circumstances and thus with dangers of all sorts.

There was also a desire to enter into the cyclical course of the cosmos in order to overcome death, and the hope of accompanying the sun god in his barque is already found here (spell 407, § 711 and spell 469, § 906); in spell 267, the deceased king goes so far as to displace the sun god from his seat in the barque, "so that this Wenis might sit in your place and row across the sky, O Re." But the identification of the king with Osiris—their identity is especially stressed in spell 219—and the many allusions to the myth of Osiris take on even greater weight, and we have here the earliest texts in which Osiris appears as ruler of the nether-world. Practically all the important motifs of the Osiris myth are found. Along with his sisters Isis and Nephthys, his son Horus also participates in the search for the murdered god (he finds him and revives him by embracing him and lifting him up [spell 364, § 612 and spell 371, § 648]), though the posthumous engendering of this son and heir is presumed in spell 366, § 632 and spell 593, §§ 1635–1636. Osiris drifts in the water, but the motif of his dismemberment by Seth is not yet attested. In spell 477, the fratricide is made subject to an accounting through a trial "be-fore the two Enneads"; although everything is denied, Horus neverthe-less wins the disputed inheritance, mourning for the murdered god comes to an end, and joy and laughter return (spell 672, § 1989).

Even if the entire corpus is not to be interpreted as ritual, a number of ritual texts nevertheless stand out, such as the Opening of the Mouth and the offering and statue rituals. Ritual spells accompany the delivery of offerings and the gifts of ointments, incense, clothing, and jewelry as well as the components of the royal regalia, particularly the crowns.

THE COFFIN TEXTS

Sources

The Coffin Texts superseded the Pyramid Texts at the end of the Old Kingdom, though some of the pyramid spells continued to be used on coffins during the Middle Kingdom. Spells from the new redaction are already found in the pyramid of King Ibi of Dynasty 8. The earliest exemplars are preserved in the necropolis of Balat in el-Kharga Oasis, if their dating to the end of the Old Kingdom is accurate. The principal sources are the later cemeteries of the nomarchs of Middle Egypt in Dynasty 12, especially Asyut, Beni Hasan, Deir el-Bersha, el-Lisht, and Meir, though on the whole, finds range from the delta to Aswan. A prominent center, yielding the largest number of spells, is Deir el-Bersha, the cemetery of Hermopolis, city of the god Thoth. The textual tradition came to an end with the conclusion of the Middle Kingdom, transforming into the new corpus of the Book of the Dead in Dynasty 17, although there are also sporadic attestations of Coffin Text spells in the New Kingdom, as in the burial chamber of Minnakhte (TT 87) and in tombs of Dynasties 25–26, when spells 151, 607, and 625 were popular. In the Middle Kingdom, the spells are encountered mainly on coffins of officials and their subordinates, though they also appear on tomb walls, stelae, canopic chests, mummy masks, and papyri.

Research

The first copies were published by C. R. Lepsius in 1867, from coffins in Berlin. After a few further publications of individual coffins, Pierre Lacau published the Middle Kingdom coffins in the Cairo Museum as a part of its *Catalogue générale* in 1904–1906, and on the basis of this material, he published individual spells in a series of articles entitled "Textes religieux" in *Receuil de travaux* 26 (1904) to 37 (1915), with the texts reproduced in a hieroglyphic type font. After World War I, James Henry Breasted and Alan H. Gardiner laid plans for a comprehensive publication of the entire corpus of texts, and this was finally realized by Adriaan de Buck in a publication consisting of seven volumes dating from 1935 to 1961. The present-day division of the spells rests on his edition, though the material has since been increased through new finds.

Early evaluations were made by James Henry Breasted (1912) and Hermann Kees (1926), both on the basis of Lacau's "Textes religieux." A French translation of the first two volumes of de Buck's edition by Louis Speleers appeared in 1947. The first complete translation in English was published by Raymond O. Faulkner (1973–1978), and there is also a complete translation in French by Paul Barguet (1986); Faulkner followed de Buck's sequence of spells, whereas Barguet edited them into thematic groups. There is as yet no translation into German.

The Book of the Two Ways, in particular, gained attention early on. Hans Schack-Schackenburg published the floor of the coffin of Sen in 1903, and Kees included a detailed treatment of its contents in his 1926 volume; several complete translations have followed in more recent times (see the bibliography; Edmund Hermsen gives a detailed survey of the history of research in the work cited there.)

Structure and Language

The division of the corpus into 1,185 spells rests on the edition of de Buck. Coffins found in a wide variety of places are collected in this edition, though many of the spells are attested in only one locale. This local element distinguishes the Coffin Texts from the other corpora. Though the language is uniformly classical Middle Egyptian, with no signs of local peculiarities, there is frequent imitation of Old Egyptian. The spells are written in vertical columns, in cursive hieroglyphs or early hieratic; they are sometimes provided with glosses or, sporadically, with what the texts call "other versions." As a rule, the titles of spells are located at their beginning, though they are also sometimes at the end. To save space, split columns are often employed for parallel expressions. Red ink is used for emphasis and to indicate divisions, and certain important spells, such as spell 1,087, are written entirely in red. The deceased is almost always spoken of in the first person singular.

In contrast to the Pyramid Texts, the Coffin Texts employ vignettes, though only rarely, and there are detailed plans in the Book of the Two Ways (figure 3) and of the Field of Offerings. In certain cases, such as in spells 81 and 100, there are descriptions of figures that were supposed to strengthen the spells' magical effect. The most detailed composition is the Book of the Two Ways, which Paul Barguet breaks up into four parts, though Leonard H. Lesko and E. Hermsen divide it into nine sections; section VII consists of a single spell (1,099) and belongs rather to section VI, given its content, as Hermsen has noted. This book, whose original title was perhaps Guide to the Ways of Rosetau and which was said to have been discovered "under the flank of Thoth," can be divided into a long version (spells 1,029–1,130) and a short version (spells 1,131–1,185, along with 513 and 577).

Content

The Coffin Texts eliminated the royal exclusivity of the Pyramid Texts, putting the texts at the disposal of all deceased persons and thus making the enjoyment of the afterlife something that all could attain; now, every deceased person was an Osiris NN. But the principal group to make use of the texts consisted of the nomarchs of the early second millennium B.C.E. and their families. The essential content of the Pyramid Texts continued, in particular the material bases for continued existence (this purpose was also served by the friezes of objects of burial goods pictured on the coffins and by spell 472, the ushabti spell, whose intent was the avoidance of compulsory labor in the afterlife), protection against inimical beings and other dangers, and admission into the cyclical course of the sun. In addition, transformation spells (inter alia, spells 268–295) dealt with the deceased king's ascent to the sky in the desirable form of a bird but also served to transform the deceased into various deities (spell 290: "into every god into which one might desire to transform"); into fire, air, or grain; or into a child or crocodile. Indeed, in this period, the most popular amulet was the scarab beetle, the hieroglyphic symbol for "transformation."

Another new motif was the desired reunion with loved ones—encountering one's own family in the afterlife. Also new was the figure of Apophis, the enemy of the sun, a gigantic serpent that had to be combated

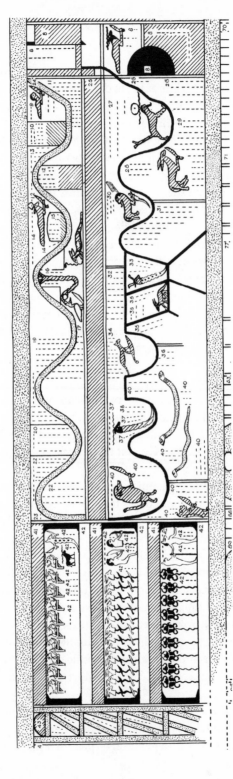

3. A portion of the Book of the Two Ways. After Adriaan de Buck, *The Egyptian Coffin Texts*, vol. 7. *Texts of Spells 787–1185*, Oriental Institute Publication 87 (Chicago, 1961), Plan I: Drawing of coffin B1C[AuQ1]. Courtesy of the Oriental Institute of The University of Chicago.

to prevent the sun's course from coming to a halt. Triumph over all enemies was now intensified into the concept of a Judgment of the Dead, to which all were subjected and which was not conducted only on indictment. Concepts of creation play a role in a number of spells, for the deceased often appears as primeval god and creator; a series of spells revolves around the constellation of the creator god and his "children," Shu and Tefnut, who carried on the work of creation. On the whole, the afterlife is conceptualized more concretely than in the Pyramid Texts, and its dangers are portrayed more dramatically. Osiris and his realm also stand out more prominently, with the deceased appearing sometimes as Osiris and sometimes as his helper and supporter, but often also in the role of his devoted son Horus who rushes to his father's assistance, as in the dramatic spell 312.

Of special importance is the Book of the Two Ways, preserved in two versions; it is the earliest example of a cosmography, though it still lacks the clear arrangement of the later Books of the Netherworld. Hermann Kees felt that it originated in "the witch's brew of magic" and the "superstitious fantasies of the people," but to the high functionaries of the Hare nome, for whose coffins it was intended, the book represented the results of government-funded research into the hereafter and was supposed to convey to the dead the knowledge necessary for them to make their way there without going astray. Its texts are always addressed directly to the deceased, warning them—or, positively, guiding them—and the schematic plans that accompany the texts were supposed to facilitate their orientation, making the book the first real guide to the hereafter, even though it lacks the systematization of the New Kingdom guides.

The Book of the Two Ways does not commence with sunset, as do the later Books of the Netherworld, but rather with the eastern horizon and sunrise, so that the journey through the hereafter takes place mainly in the sky. Many obstacles and dangers stand in the way of the deceased, such as the circle of fire (designated the "fiery court") around the sun and the menacing guardians at the gates of the hereafter. Pitch-black darkness or walls of flame also constantly block the way. In the middle of this description of the hereafter is the region of Rosetau, which lies "at the boundary of the sky" and contains the corpse of Osiris; according to spell 1,080, it is "locked in darkness and surrounded by fire." The deceased wishes to reach this place, for whoever gazes on the deceased Osiris cannot die (CT VII 302e). Another goal is the Field of Offerings with its paradisiacal superabundance, but the route leading to it is patently difficult, and near the end of the book, we encounter paths that cross one another and lead nowhere. The Lake of Flames situated between the Two Ways is an ambivalent place whose consuming fire also serves the purpose of regeneration. The creation of a system of gateways in the hereafter was attempted with the seven guardians in spells 1,100–1,110. In the center of the last section are three boats, all perhaps intended to be the solar barque, from which the serpent Apophis is repelled. The Lord of All speaks his concluding monologue (spell 1,130) from this barque, recounting his beneficent deeds when he created the world and foretelling the end of this creation after "millions of years"; only he and Osiris will survive the end of time.

In general, the netherworld and its ruler, Osiris, gained greatly in importance, though the celestial afterlife of the Pyramid Texts survives, as in the astronomical representations on the lids of coffins at Asyut, with their decans and stars from the northern celestial regions, and in the person of the sky goddess, Nut. In the Book of the Two Ways as well, a plurality of skies appears as the goal of deceased persons, who are ever and again supplied with the knowledge necessary to avoid dangers and false paths. In dialogues with the guardians of the gateways, the deceased employ this knowledge to establish their legitimacy.

THE BOOK OF THE DEAD

Sources

The Book of the Dead is the designation of a group of mortuary spells, written mostly on papyrus, from the New Kingdom, the Third Intermediate Period, and the Late Period. In the later versions of the Coffin Texts, some spells already take the form of the corresponding spells in the New Kingdom Book of the Dead. Early examples of spells from the Book of the Dead are found on mummy cloths and coffins of the early New Kingdom, and somewhat later, they appear on papyri and on the walls of certain tomb chambers. Early examples, once ascribed to the Middle Kingdom (the coffins of Mentuhotpe and Herunefer, and a papyrus now in Brussels), are now dated to Dynasty 17. The collection circulated throughout Egypt, though Thebes was an especially important center. Spells from the Book of the Dead began to be used rather commonly by officials beginning with the reign of Tuthmosis III. The production of Books of the Dead was briefly interrupted by the Amarna Period, though a number of spells are found once again on the gilded shrines of Tutankhamun and on other objects from his tomb, while many important manuscripts stem from the period of transition to the Ramesside era. The Book of the Dead started to appear on the walls of royal tombs in the reign of Merneptah, beginning with spell 125, which deals with the Judgment of the Dead; though it was supplemented by other texts in the royal tombs of Dynasty 20, the spell nevertheless remained the most important one. Some spells occur on temple walls,

such as spell 148, and also spell 110 at Medinet Habu. The chapters regarding the heart—spells 26–30, but especially spell 30B, and occasionally spell 6 (there is an example in Dresden) and 126 (at Tanis)—were
employed on scarabs.

In Dynasty 21, and occasionally already in the Ramesside Period,
some Books of the Dead were written in hieratic, though papyri also
continued to be written with cursive hieroglyphs. They were now often
enclosed in a statuette of Osiris; when possible, a Book of the Dead and
an Amduat papyrus were employed together, while less often, mixed
forms combined elements from both compositions. In certain pictorial
versions called mythological papyri, Book of the Dead spells are represented only by their vignettes. After Dynasty 22, Books of the Dead fell
into disuse for a time, but Dynasty 26 saw a revival of their employment, along with new spells and a canonization of their order. The spells
also reappeared on tomb walls and coffins at this time and, beginning
with Dynasty 30, on mummy bandages. This new flowering continued
into the Roman Period, from which a version written in Demotic has
also been preserved. Spells 19, 140, 157, 158, and 162–165 are attested
only after the New Kingdom.

As a continuation of the Coffin Texts, this collection of spells was
available to everyone, and it was in widespread use among royal officials and members of their families. Even after the development of a
new corpus of Books of the Afterlife for royal use, beginning with the
Amduat and the Litany of Re, certain spells were adopted for use on elements of the royal tomb furnishings; an important example of this is the
shroud of Tuthmosis III, and the treasure of Tutankhamun offers a number of others. With Merneptah begins the use of spells—at first 125, and
later others as well—on the walls of the royal tombs.

Illustrations

At first, only in certain cases and for special emphasis did spells include a vignette, that is, a symbolic representation summarizing the intent or the content of a spell in concise pictorial form supplementing
what is stated in the texts. Thus, in the burial chamber of Minnakhte
(TT 87) from the reign of Tuthmosis III, only two of a total of thirty-five
spells are illustrated, but by the Ramesside Period, only a few spells remain without a vignette. In Dynasty 21 and in the Late Period, the vignettes are often used as abbreviations for entire spells, appearing without the accompanying texts. In many manuscripts, the vignettes
constitute a row of pictures, with the texts placed underneath them. The

colophons of individual spells often make reference to accompanying illustrations that are supposed to be executed according to specific instructions. From the New Kingdom to the Late Period, the vignettes were brightly painted, whereas those of the Ptolemaic and Roman Periods made no use of color.

Research

Some manuscripts were published as early as 1821, in volume 2 of the *Description de l'Égypte* prepared by Napoleon Bonaparte's expedition, and a Ptolemaic example had been reproduced even earlier, by Jean Marcel Cadet in 1805. Jean-François Champollion concerned himself with further Books of the Dead in Geneva and Turin, for which he employed the designation *rituel funéraire* ("funerary ritual"). In 1842, Karl Richard Lepsius published the Ptolemaic Period manuscript in Turin, introducing the term *Totenbuch* ("Book of the Dead") and the numbering of the chapters that remains in use to this day. In 1872, Théodule Dévéria published the papyrus of Nebqed in Paris, with a translation by Paul Pierret, after Samuel Birch had already published the first English translation, based on the papyrus in Turin, in 1867. The first German translation by Heinrich Brugsch in *ZÄS* 10 (1872) was only a partial one.

In 1874, the publication of a complete edition was decided on at the Second Congress of Orientalists in London, and the project was placed in the hands of Edouard Naville of Geneva. Because of the amount of material, Naville was obliged to confine himself to manuscripts from the New Kingdom, of which he included seventy-one. His three-volume work appeared in 1886, and it remains the standard edition to this day. In a parallel effort, W. Willem Pleyte published additional spells from manuscripts of the Late Period in 1881, continuing, as did Naville, to use the numbering of spells introduced by Lepsius, with the result that spells 166 to 174 coincide. E. A. Wallis Budge concerned himself with the manuscripts in the British Museum and published some of them, including the papyrus of Ani (for the first time in 1890), which Naville had not dealt with; Budge's text edition of 1898, in hieroglyphic type, has been continuously reprinted and is still widely used. A catalogue of manuscripts of the New Kingdom and Third Intermediate Period in the British Museum begun by Alan W. Shorter remains uncompleted, while Thomas George Allen published a catalogue of all the manuscripts in the Oriental Institute in Chicago.

Peter Le Page Renouf, whose work was continued by Naville, made an early translation; they published a complete rendering into English in

PSBA 14–26 (1892–1904). Pierret had already published a French translation in 1882, naturally without Naville's "new" spells. Budge's continuously reprinted English translation first appeared in 1901. A new standard has been set by the more recent complete translations by Barguet, Allen, Erik Hornung, and Raymond O. Faulkner, while fundamentals in understanding the texts were established by Kurt Sethe and Hermann Kees in their "Göttinger Totenbuchstudien." As early as 1887, Gaston Maspero published a detailed survey of the contents of the entire composition in *RHR* 15.

Once viewed as the Bible of the ancient Egyptians, the Book of the Dead lost a great deal of its interest to scholars with the discovery of the Pyramid Texts, though it continues to exercise great influence as witness to an esoteric Egypt. Ongoing attempts to compare it with the Tibetan Book of the Dead fail because of the entirely different objectives of the two compositions.

Structure and Language

The spells are clearly set apart from one another by titles, and sometimes also colophons, written with red ink, and they are separated in some manuscripts by double lines. Lepsius divided the Turin manuscript he used as a prototype into 165 "chapters," though the designation "spell" is undoubtedly more suitable for these ever-changing and recombined sections, especially since the term chapter is never used in connection with the older corpora. In contrast to the Coffin Texts, the stock of spells is considerably reduced to a total of less than two hundred: 186 in Naville's edition, increased to 190 by Budge. To date, we have no papyrus from the New Kingdom containing a collection of all the spells. In Ramesside tombs there occur some spell titles and vignettes that as yet have no parallels in the manuscripts (Mohamed Saleh, *Totenbuch,* pp. 90–94; see the bibliography).

On the papyri, and in part on tomb walls, use is made of a cursive form of hieroglyphs (*Totenbuch-Kursiv*) that stands somewhere between hieratic and actual hieroglyphs. In the tomb of Khaemhet from the reign of Amenophis III, a version of spell 85 appears in "enigmatic" writing. The language continues to be classical Middle Egyptian.

The collection of spells was originally designated the Book (or Spells) of Coming Out by Day. Before the Ptolemaic Period, no obligatory sequence of spells prevailed, though there were certain preferences; thus, in the New Kingdom, spell 1 or 17 was preferred at the beginning, and 149 and 150 at the end (this was also true in Dynasty 21, often combined with a representation of the course of the sun), though spells 110 and 186 were also popular at the end in the Ramesside Period. The canonical sequence, in which certain spells were grouped together, was in large part formed in Dynasty 26. Doublets of the same spell occur in many manuscripts. The number of spells employed varies considerably: the papyrus of Kha in Turin contains 33, Yuya's 41, Ani's 65, and that of Nu in London 137. The length of the spells also fluctuates, from a few verses to nearly four hundred in the case of spell 17 and its glosses. Many spells are provided with colophons containing concrete instructions on their use or application, or notations concerning their desired usefulness.

Content

Like the two earlier text corpora, the Book of the Dead primarily served the purposes of provisioning and protecting the deceased. In contrast to the contemporary Books of the Netherworld, it is not concerned with descriptions but rather with practical help and magical assistance for the hereafter. The idea of a general Judgment of the Dead to which every deceased person is subject plays a central role. What clearly declines in contrast to the Coffin Texts is the wish for a reunion with the members of one's family. The most important spells are spell 1, which legitimizes the deceased as the god Thoth and further through knowledge of the mysterious events surrounding Osiris; spell 6, the *ushabti* spell, which activates this assistant to the deceased; spell 15, which contains a hymn to the sun, selected from a large repertoire; spell 16, the vignette to spell 15 (figure 4); spell 17, which identifies the deceased with the creator god, Atum, and offers a synopsis of the entire Book of the Dead, provided with explanatory glosses, and which was especially richly illustrated after the Amarna Period; spell 18, also provided with glosses, which allows the deceased to prevail over opponents before any divine tribunal; spell 25, which prevents forgetting one's name; spells 26–30, dealing with the heart, which must be in harmony with the deceased; spells 31 and 32, directed against crocodiles in the hereafter; spells 33–35, against snakes; spell 38, which guarantees the breath of life, as do 54–56; spells 39 and 108, which deal with the battle against Apophis, the enemy of the sun; spell 40, which wards off "him who swallowed an ass"; spell 42, which contains a deification of the body parts of the dead, so that, member by member, the deceased becomes a god; spell 44, which prevents "dying again in the necropolis"; spell 45, which prevents putrefaction; spells 51–53, which prevent a reversal of the digestive process in the afterlife, as do spells 82, 102, 124, and 189; spells 57–63, which guarantee

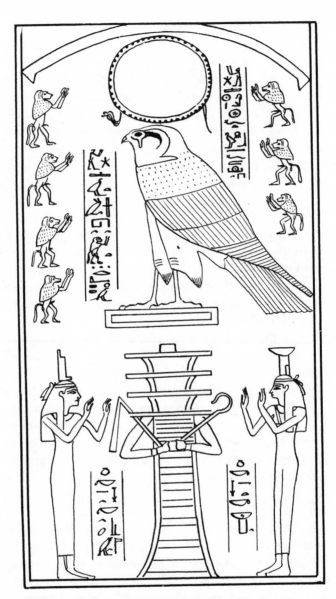

4. Vignette to Book of the Dead spell 16. After Edouard Naville, *Das Ägyptische Todtenbuch der XVIII. bis XX. Dynastie*, vol. I (Berlin, 1886), plate XXII.

5. Vignette to Book of the Dead spell 89. After Edouard Naville, *Das Ägyptische Todtenbuch der XVIII. bis XX. Dynastie,* vol. I (Berlin, 1886), plate CI.

air and water in the realm of the dead; spell 59, which addresses the sycamore tree of the goddess Nut and accompanies a depiction of the tree goddess; the barely comprehensible spell 64, which attempts to summarize the entire book in a single spell; spell 71, which attempts to release the deceased from the necropolis and requests continued life; spell 72, especially popular on coffins, which was supposed to fulfill all material needs, and the similar spell 106; spells 76–88, which serve to transform the deceased into various forms, such as a falcon (77–78), the god Atum (79) or the god Ptah (82), a lotus blossom (81), a *benu*-heron (83), the *ba* (soul) of Re (85), a swallow (86), a serpent (87), and a crocodile (88). Spell 89 serves to reunite the *ba* and the corpse in the afterlife (figure 5); spells 91 and 92 permit free, unhindered movement; spell 94 provides the deceased with writing material; spells 98 and 99 assure a ferryboat in the realm of the dead, and spell 99 contains a lengthy dialogue with the ferryman and the parts of his boat. Spells 100–102 effect the inclusion of the deceased in the journey of the sun god in his barque, as do 130, 133, 134, and 136; spell 103 projects the deceased into the following of Hathor; spell 104 allows the deceased to "dwell among the great gods"; in spell 105, the deceased is presented with *ka* (life force). Spells 107–109 and 111–116 serve to assure knowledge of the *bau* (souls), while spell 108 is again concerned with the warding off of Apophis by the god Seth. Spell 110 describes the Field of Offerings or Field of Reeds as a paradise for the blessed dead; spells 117–119 deal with free entry into Rosetau, the realm of Osiris; spell 124 prepares the deceased for the descent to the "tribunal of Osiris"; and spell 125 is the central spell of the Judgment of the Dead, with its denial of sin (the Negative Confession) on the part of the dead (figure 6); the complementary spell 126 again refers to the Lake of Fire and its guardians. Spells 127

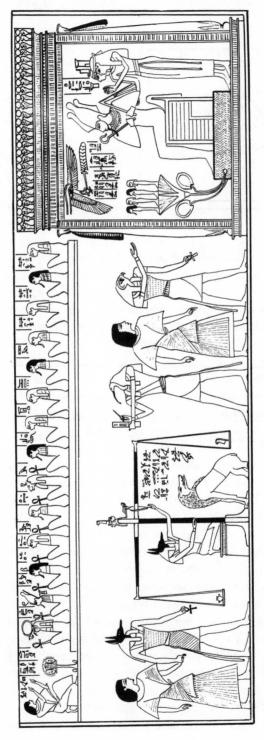

6. Vignette to Book of the Dead spell 125. After Edouard Naville, *Das Ägyptische Todtenbuch der XVIII. bis XX. Dynastie*, vol. I (Berlin, 1886), plate CXXXVI.

7. Vignette to Book of the Dead spell 153. After Edouard Naville, *Das Ägyptische Todtenbuch der XVIII. bis XX. Dynastie*, vol. I (Berlin, 1886), plate CLXXVIII.

and 180 adopt portions of the royal Litany of Re. Spell 137 is concerned with the illumination of the hereafter in the absence of sun and moon, and in spell 138, the deceased as Horus greets the deities of Abydos. Spells 141–143 contain an offering litany with a long list of deities and forms of manifestations of Osiris, who are to take part in the offerings. Spells 144–147 are concerned with the gateways of the hereafter, which are seven or twenty-one in number, and their menacing guardians, whom the deceased may pass only by knowing their names and reciting the correct spells; spell 148, with its seven cows and four rudders of the sky, assures the nourishment of the deceased, while spell 149 describes the fourteen hills in the realm of the dead, which are again enumerated in spell 150 in their characteristic form. Spell 151 displays the most important elements of the funeral, with Anubis standing by the bier in the center. Spell 152 assures the deceased a secure place among the "millions" who dwell in the hereafter; spell 153 protects the dead from the giant net spread out between sky and earth (figure 7); spell 154 helps to overcome the perishing of the corpse. Spells 155–160 belong to certain effective amulets; spell 161, very popular on coffins, assures the deceased the necessary breath of life; spell 162 belongs to a panel placed under the head of the mummy, spell 166 to the headrest, and spell 167 to the *udjat*-amulet. Spell 168 is discussed later in this volume under the Books of the Netherworld as the Spell of the Twelve Caves. In spell 171, all the gods and goddesses are supposed to give "pure clothing" to the deceased, while spell 172 again deifies the entire body of the deceased. In spell 173, the deceased as Horus greets Osiris; spell 175 contains the well-known dialogue between Atum and Osiris concerning the hereafter; chapter 176 affords protection against the dangerous east and its "Place of Destruction," which brings a "second death"; and spells 177

8. Vignette to Book of the Dead spell 186. After Edouard Naville, *Das Ägyptische Todten-buch der XVIII. bis XX. Dynastie*, vol. I (Berlin, 1886), plate CCXII.

and 178 collect age-old Pyramid Text spells concerned with ascending to the sky. Spell 179 is directed against enemies; spells 181 and 183–185 are hymns to Osiris; spell 182 serves to protect and regenerate the deceased, who reappears as Thoth here; and spell 186 contains an adoration of Hathor in the form of a cow (figure 8).

THE BOOKS OF BREATHING

Sources

Nearly all the preserved copies of the Books of Breathing date to the Greco-Roman Period; the earliest, P. Louvre N 3154, stems from the end of Dynasty 30 (c. 350 B.C.E.). The Egyptians distinguished between a First and a Second Book of Breathing, with the second preserved only from the Roman Period. Both books make reference to divine origin—the first was supposed to have been written by Isis for Osiris, and the second to have been copied by Thoth, who was believed to have authored other works as well. In all instances, the earthly origin of these texts was in Thebes, where they were composed and handed down by the priesthood of Amun. Jean-Claude Goyon has pointed to certain parallels to passages from the Books of Breathing in the texts of the Buchis bull stelae from Armant, near Thebes.

Research

Vivant Denon published a manuscript in 1804; it served as the basis for Heinrich Brugsch's 1851 treatment, which was written in Latin. Philippe Jacques de Horrack, relying on several papyri in the Louvre, published an edition of the first book in 1877. The litany of names from the fourth text of the second book (see "Content" section of this chapter) was published as a separate composition by Jens D. C. Lieblein in 1895. In more recent times, Goyon in particular has promoted the study of this text.

Structure and Language

The original title is better translated as Document of Breathing, though the designation "book" has become accepted on the analogy of the title Book of the Dead. Goyon divided the first book into fifteen (perhaps originally only twelve) sections. These yield a relatively unified composition, whereas the second book consists of texts with highly varied content. Additionally, there exist various abbreviated versions of the second and fourth parts of this second book. All copies of both books known to date are written in hieratic; only a few abbreviated versions are in the Demotic script. P. Louvre N 3284 has vignettes as well.

Content

Both books stress the importance of breath for the deceased. They serve to prolong the existence of the name of the deceased and to prevent the "second death" of damnation. In contrast to the Book of the Dead, Amun plays an important role here, especially, in one group of abbreviated versions, as Amenemope, that is, Amun of Luxor. But it is Osiris who assures the survival of the *ba*, and the texts are supposed to serve the deceased as a sort of identity card in the realm of the dead, with the result that they belong to the genre of divine decrees.

Purification, intactness of the body, and the vindication of the deceased are the focus of the first book, whose goal is the deceased's continued existence. They breathe and see, the doors of the hereafter are open to them, offerings are made to them, and so forth; every place stands open to their *bas*. In section thirteen, we find a variant of the Negative Confession, and the merits of the deceased are emphasized in a positive manner in section fourteen.

According to Goyon, the second book consists of six very different texts. The first has to do with the deceased's coffin and the materials of which it is made; in the second, the doorkeepers and guardians of the netherworld are addressed, so that the deceased might pass by them; to that end, the deceased assumes the role of various deities. A rather long address to Thoth is a variant on Book of the Dead spells 18–20 regarding the "wreath of vindication"; a "deification of the limbs" has to do with the desired corporal integrity and the power to make use of all the parts of the body. The third text contains addresses to the deities of the hereafter and a request for the issuing of a "document of breathing," and the fourth is a litany for the protection of the deceased's name. The fifth text is based on Book of the Dead spell 162, the spell regarding the plaque placed under the head, as well as spell 72, here much altered. The sixth ends with an address to Nut as mother of the deceased, the latter appearing in the role of Osiris.

Among texts with related content, a papyrus in Parma (number 107; see pp. 314–317 of the work by Goyon cited in the bibliography) represents itself as a Book of Admission into the Realm of the Dead and Arrival at the Hall of Maat, where the Judgment of the Dead takes place.

THE NEW KINGDOM BOOKS
OF THE NETHERWORLD

General

In the New Kingdom, parallel to the development of the Coffin Texts into the Book of the Dead, a new, almost purely royal literary genre was created: in Egyptian, it was designated (Books of) What Is in the Duat (the Netherworld). In modern times, these works were at first referred to as Guides to the Hereafter, but the name Books of the Netherworld (or Underworld) is now generally accepted in English. The German equivalent is *Unterweltsbücher*, and in French, they are called *Livres du monde inférieur* or the like. These are the first religious books that are not ever-changing collections of spells, as the Book of the Dead still was; instead, these have permanent, unchanging content. Additionally, their pictures are not separate vignettes but rather constitute, along with the text, a solid unity. With few exceptions, these thoroughly illustrated books were handed down only by royalty until Dynasty 21 and could not even be used by queens, as shown by the tomb of Nofretari.

A clear formal distinction exists between the earlier Books of the Netherworld—the Amduat and the Book of Gates—and the later ones. The earlier compositions are arranged according to the twelve hours of the night, with the barque conveying the sun god in his ram-headed, nocturnal form placed in the center of each hour. In the later books, the solar barque is almost entirely absent; instead, the presence of the god is indicated by his red sun disk, which is absent, however, from scenes depicting the damned. In the Book of Caverns, the twelvefold division according to the hours is replaced by an arrangement into six sectors, while the division in the Book of the Earth has yet to be explained.

Formally, compositions such as the Litany of Re and the Book of the Heavenly Cow differ considerably from the Books of the Netherworld; in particular, they are not thoroughly illustrated. Their content is quite similar, however, especially that of the Litany of Re, with its nocturnal, otherworldly forms of manifestation of the sun god, and their intended effect in the netherworld.

The nightly journey of the sun is the focus of all the Books of the Netherworld, and consistent with this, it also furnishes the ordering and creative principle for the spaces in the hereafter. This nocturnal regeneration of the sun demonstrates, by way of example, what powers of renewal are at work on the far side of death. At the same time, the journey occurs in the spaces of the human soul, in which a renewal from the depths becomes possible. That it is an odyssey of the soul is emphasized by the Egyptians through the indication that the sun god descends into the depths as a *ba*-soul (and thus is ram-headed, since *ba* is also the word for ram); herein lie significant antecedents of modern psychotherapy. The nocturnal journey leads through an inner region of the cosmos (what the German poet Rainer Maria Rilke has referred to as *Weltinnenraum*) that was regarded not only as the netherworld and the depths of the earth, but also as water (the primeval water, called Nun), as darkness, and as the interior of the sky. Connected to this are the symbolic representations, so popular from the Amarna Period on, that attempt to summarize the entire course of the sun in a single, complex picture.

We will discuss the books here in the chronological order in which they were presumably composed.

The Amduat
Sources

It is possible that the oldest fragments of the Amduat, which are from the tomb of Tuthmosis I, actually belong to the early years of Queen Hatshepsut, for we must reckon with a reburial of the king by his daughter. But earlier accounts, according to which a portion of these fragments stem from the tomb of Hatshepsut (KV 20), are improbable; they clearly constitute a unity and can scarcely be apportioned to two tombs. Hartwig Altenmüller assumes "various stages of composition" before Tuthmosis I, leading back "perhaps to the Old Kingdom," but such a detailed description of the netherworld, with its quantity of illustrations, is entirely unimaginable for the Old Kingdom and highly unlikely even for the Middle Kingdom. Nevertheless, even at present, the book continues to be dated to before the New Kingdom, despite the lack of any thorough rationale for such an estimation.

Our earliest complete copies stem from the tomb of Tuthmosis III and that of Useramun, the first of his viziers. Both take into account the text's own notes regarding orientation and attempt to distribute the hours of the night according to the four cardinal points (see "Content" in this section), with the beginning of the text in the west and its end in the east, although the relatively small wall surfaces of Useramun's tomb necessitated a modification of the distribution. Amenophis II did not take the prescribed orientation into account but rather placed all the hours in a purely sequential order, with the short version of the composition (see "Content") at its end. Tuthmosis IV left his sarcophagus chamber undecorated, whereas Amenophis III again had the Amduat as the standard decoration on the walls of his sarcophagus chamber, with the hours in sequential order and the abbreviated version at the end.

After the reign of Akhenaten, when provisions were made for the burials of Tutankhamun and Aya, the Amduat was minimally represented by selections from the first hour; in the tomb of Tutankhamun, two additional (incomplete) hours were placed on one of his gilded shrines. Haremhab, on the other hand, followed by Ramesses I, completely abandoned the Amduat and chose the later version of the Book of Gates for his sarcophagus chamber. Because the shrines from these and the remaining royal tombs are lost to us, it remains uncertain whether the Amduat continued to be used on their walls.

With Sethos I, the Amduat returned to the walls of the sarcophagus chamber; the first three hours surround the sarcophagus while the continuation is scattered throughout the tomb. From this time down through the reign of Ramesses III, the fourth and fifth hours had a permanent place in the third corridor and the location of the remaining hours varied, and from Merneptah on, there was no longer an Amduat in the sarcophagus chamber. The twelfth hour, which is lacking in Sethos I's tomb, is represented by two versions in the tomb of Ramesses II, one of them in the shaft (figure 9), which is otherwise without parallel. The short version, which Sethos had placed around his sarcophagus, had a subsidiary chamber of its own reserved for it in the tomb of Ramesses II; it was omitted in the tombs that followed, and only in Dynasty 21 did it reappear on papyri. Because the material is lacking,

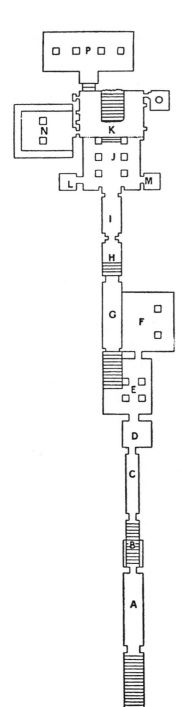

9. Layout of a typical New Kingdom royal tomb, as illustrated by a plan of the tomb of Sethos I. A, first corridor; B, second corridor; C, third corridor; D, shaft; E, first pillared hall; F, side chamber; G–H, lower corridors; I, antechamber; J, sarcophagus chamber; K, "crypt"; L–O, side chambers; P, end room. After E. Hornung and E. Staehelin, Sethos—ein Pharaonengrab (Basel, 1991), p. 44.

we cannot say to what extent texts from the Amduat were represented on the gilded shrines or on other portions of the tomb furnishings in the royal tombs of the Ramesside Period; in the case of Sethos I in particular, we could assume that the otherwise missing twelfth hour was represented. No New Kingdom papyri contain the Amduat.

Down to Ramesses III, all the royal tombs display extensive excerpts from the Amduat. Ramesses IV then took a new direction, contenting himself with a few citations from the short and long versions. Ramesses VI, however, had a relatively complete exemplar, for the first time since Dynasty 18, in the fourth and fifth corridors of his tomb, where the hours are once again in sequential order, though with transpositions and abbreviations of the contents of the seventh through the eleventh hours, while the twelfth hour is absent. Ramesses IX limited himself to the second hour and a part of the third, as well as a citation (the corpse of the sun from the sixth hour) in his sarcophagus chamber.

In the latter part of Dynasty 21, on the analogy of the Pyramid Texts, a democratization of the book ensued; at Thebes, the priests of Amun adopted it for their coffins and papyri, and in Dynasty 22, the high priest Iuput used it in his cenotaph at Abydos. With very few exceptions, the papyri from this period contain only the last four hours of the night and the short version. Their layout varies considerably: the contents of the individual hours are sometimes abbreviated and intermingled, or even enriched by additional pictorial elements, and instead of the usual three registers (i.e., rows of depictions; see "Content"), they are sometimes arranged into two registers or only a single one. Usage decreased to only a few motifs in Dynasty 22 but gained fresh dimensions in Dynasty 26, at first on the walls of tombs of officials (Petamenophis, fragments from Roda) and then on royal and nonroyal sarcophagi of Dynasty 30 and the early Ptolemaic Period. Thus, the sarcophagus of Nectanebo II, which was never used because of the king's flight from the Persians in 343 B.C.E., was decorated with a selection of six hours from the Amduat; in the case of Wereshnefer (MMA 14.7.1), only the eighth hour is lacking, and in that of Berlin 49, only the twelfth hour.

Beyond this series of sarcophagi, parts of the Amduat can be tracked down on wooden coffins from the early Ptolemaic Period. Examples are the coffin from the tomb shaft of Basa (TT 389), with the first and eighth hours, and some figures on the coffin of Harendotes (BM 6678), which is dated to the reign of Ptolemy III. The contents of the texts and figures—which were often copied more faithfully in the late exemplars than in the Ramesside Period—were in and of themselves unchangeable, though doors guarded by serpents were added to the individual hours of the night on several late sarcophagi.

Research

Jean-François Champollion mentioned the Amduat only in his description of the tomb of Amenophis III, where he was struck by its cursive version, in the thirteenth of his letters from Egypt; but he copied texts and representations from this book in other tombs, thus laying the foundation for its study. In addition, in 1879 Ridolfo V. Lanzone published the first Turin papyrus containing the Amduat. Pioneering though incomplete was the translation and analysis by Gaston Maspero in 1888, which served as a foundation for Alfred Wiedemann, Edouard Naville, E. A. Wallis Budge, and others; a fresh and complete French translation was eventually prepared by Gilles Roulin. In 1894, Gustave Jéquier published and translated the short version, though he could take into consideration only a single version from the New Kingdom—that of Sethos I—for the tombs of Tuthmosis III and Amenophis II were not discovered until 1898. Eugène Lefébure's highly imperfect copy from the tomb of Sethos I, published in 1886, served for many years as the basic edition of the long version and was employed in the preparation of the *Wörterbuch der ägyptischen Sprache* (Dictionary of the Egyptian Language). Budge supplied detailed descriptions of individual hours of the night in *The Gods of the Egyptians* (1904) and *The Egyptian Heaven and Hell* (1905), with translations. Paul Bucher published the concluding texts of the first three hours in 1931, though in hieroglyphic type and only according to the three versions of Tuthmosis III, Amenophis II, and Sethos I; in the following year, he published the tombs of Tuthmosis III and Amenophis II in *MIFAO* 60, with photographs and the texts in hieroglyphic type, thus broadening the textual basis.

Alexandre Piankoff's publication of the tomb of Ramesses VI in 1954 represented a further step, and the English translation he included has yet to be superseded. In 1963 appeared Erik Hornung's edition of the long version (and, in 1967, the short version), with the first translation into German; these were replaced by a synoptic edition by the same author, *Texte zum Amduat* (1987–1994). Since these editions include only versions from the New Kingdom, A. F. Sadek's 1985 publication of papyri with copies of the Amduat in the Cairo Museum represents an important supplement. With regard to the meaning of the compositions,

A. Schweitzer published an interpretation from a psychoanalytic point of view in 1994.

Structure and Language

As an individual Book of the Netherworld, the Amduat bears an original title, namely, Book of the Hidden Chamber; the modern designation Amduat ("that which is in the Duat") stems from the Egyptian name for all the Books of the Netherworld. Its division into twelve sections corresponds to the twelve hours of the night. Each hour except the first has a heading, written horizontally, that summarily describes significant events that occur in the hour, along with remarks concerning its usefulness and its orientation (see "Content"). Additionally, a brief introduction in vertical columns gives the names of the hour, its gateways, and its region of the netherworld and serves as a clear division between one hour and the next. Only the first three hours have lengthy concluding texts as well. Special insertions such as those that would become customary beginning with the Book of Gates are absent, and the concluding scene depicting the arms of Shu and the sun is not yet separated from the twelfth hour.

The Amduat is the first completely illustrated book; the texts and pictures constitute a unity and the texts make constant reference to the illustrations. Unfinished portions in the tombs of Haremhab and Sethos II show that first the scenes were copied onto the walls and then their accompanying texts. The representations and their captions are arranged in three registers, with the solar barque always appearing in the middle one. This register also includes the central theme of the hour, while the upper register is devoted to general phenomena in the netherworld and the lower register treats further motifs specific to the region of the hour. Exceptional features are offered in the first hour, with its doubling of the middle register (a barque appears at the beginning of each half) and its enumerations of deities in the other two registers, and in the fourth and fifth hours, with their partially crossed registers. Only in the latter two hours are there individual captions in enigmatic writing; in the other hours, abbreviated writings that in most cases cannot be designated enigmatic often accompany the normal writings. Retrograde writing is preferred in the texts, and the representations are also mostly to be read in reverse. Unlike the later Book of Gates, where the sun barque is depicted being towed in each of the twelve hours of the night, the towing of the barque occurs here in only four of them: the fourth, fifth, eighth, and twelfth.

Notations in the individual hours distribute them according to the four cardinal directions, running along a rectangle with two hours on each of the short sides and four on each of the long sides. The only tombs that display at least an attempt to take this into account are those of Tuthmosis III and Useramun, with the directions followed exactly only in the sarcophagus chamber of the former, though in the catalogue of deities, the hours are ordered sequentially, with the solar barque always at the beginning, as was also done later in the sarcophagus chambers of Amenophis II and Amenophis III. Because of the narrowness of his burial chamber, Useramun was obliged to make changes in the distribution, in particular the displacement of two of the hours from the east to the north wall. In the tomb of Tuthmosis III, the last hour of the night lies precisely in the east, while the entrance to the sarcophagus chamber corresponds to the sandy road of the Land of Sokar.

In addition to the long, illustrated version, a short (called "abridged" by Maspero and Jéquier) version is found in the tombs and on papyri; it is appended to the book like a concluding chapter and contains no pictures. Like the long version, it is divided into twelve sections. It is a sort of abstract (*sehuy*, "summary") containing special emphases, in particular listing important names of the individual hours of the night and adding further remarks regarding usefulness. It seems to be divided metrically into 300 verses.

In the tomb of Tuthmosis III, references to the king are constantly inserted into the text of the book, a practice entirely given up by Amenophis II and Amenophis III. In the tomb of Sethos I, such references are inserted only in the concluding texts in the second corridor, while in the tombs of Dynasty 20, they occur in just a few places. In the tomb of Tuthmosis III, an exceptional instance is the catalogue of deities in the upper pillared hall (the antechamber to the sarcophagus chamber); it arranges most of the beings (though none of the enemies) who appear in the Amduat in the manner of a list but with their order occasionally modified, while the stars that are inserted in each case indicate the desired ascent of the king's *ba*-soul into the heavens.

Content

The detailed opening section of the Amduat stresses knowledge; it promises knowledge of netherworldly phenomena nine (which in Egyptian stands for "many, many") times, and in the process, it also affords a summary of the content of the Amduat. The book describes the journey of the sun god through the twelve hours of the night, from his setting to his rising in the morning. In between, we are presented with the actions and speeches of the sun god as well as with descriptions of the entities in the netherworld and their functions. It is the first religious treatise to insert the king consistently into the daily course of the sun. While Osiris is mentioned again and again and is often depicted, he remains entirely passive; in the entire Amduat, he does not speak even once. Direct reference to the deceased king is made only in the sixth hour, at the crucial moment when the *ba* of the sun unites with his corpse.

The book begins with the entry of the sun god, as a ram-headed *ba* ("soul"), into the interstitial realm of the first hour of the night, and it ends with his rebirth in the morning, after uniting with his corpse in the middle of his journey in the sixth hour and overcoming the menacing serpent Apophis in the seventh hour.

With its arrangement into lists of the various important beings in the afterlife, the first hour of the night (figure 14) lays the foundation for an ordering and unfolding of the Unknown, into which the sun descends in the evening. The solar baboons and the goddesses of the hours, along with the other deities in the upper and lower registers, personify the general rejoicing evoked by the appearance of the sun, in which all the inhabitants of the afterlife except for the "enemies" participate. In the middle register, the goddess Maat appears twice directly in front of the solar barque; later, she will appear at the beginning of the second hour, stressing that justice and law rule even here in the afterlife. In a second barque, the sun god is already present in his morning form of the scarab beetle; he is being worshiped by Osiris, who was considered to be his nocturnal form. The beginning of the journey thus already alludes to its successful completion. Personified stelae, provided with human heads, allude to the commanding power of the god, who communicates all that is necessary for those in the afterlife through his directives. At the end is the opening and the resealing of the netherworld, which is called the Great City because of its large number of inhabitants. With its gateway named Swallower of All, this posthumous world contains everything that has ever existed.

The next two hours (figures 10, 15, and 16) begin the actual netherworld, which is depicted first as a realm of abundance dominated by the watery expanse called Wernes in the second hour and by the Waters of Osiris in the third. In both hours, the solar barque is accompanied by other boats that are not depicted again in the later hours. The

10. Amduat, second and third hours, with short version above. From the tomb of Sethos I. Photography by the Egyptian Expedition, The Metropolitan Museum of Art, New York. Photo courtesy of The Metropolitan Museum of Art.

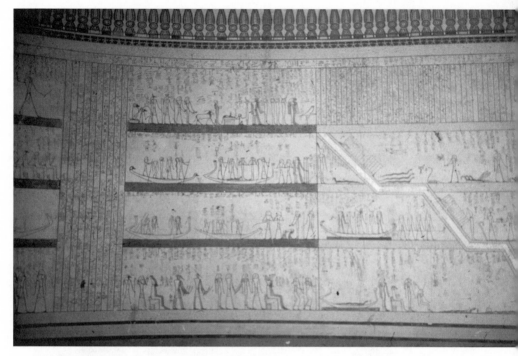

11. Amduat, third and fourth hours. From the tomb of Tuthmosis III. Photo by U. Schweitzer.

god concerns himself with assigning land to the blessed dead, who carry ears of grain in their hands or wear them in their hair in the lower register. These are the peasants of Wernes, and provision for their material needs is the theme here. The presence of Osiris manifests itself a number of times in the lower register of the third hour, and in the text that concludes the hour, Re is even said to turn and face him directly. We also encounter avenging creatures with knives in hand to render all enemies harmless.

This well-watered, abundant landscape ends at the fourth hour (figures 11 and 17). Here lies the desert of Rosetau, the "Land of Sokar, who is on his sand," a desolate, sandy realm teeming with snakes whose uncanny movement is emphasized by the legs and wings on their bodies. A zigzag route filled with fire and repeatedly blocked by doors leads through the region of this hour. For the first time, the solar barque needs to be towed for it to make progress, and the barque itself turns into a serpent whose fiery breath pierces a pathway through the otherwise impenetrable gloom. In the very middle of this darkly menacing hour, Horus and Sokar look after the solar Eye, protecting and renewing it, while at the end we are afforded an unexpected and consoling glimpse of the morning sky.

The structure of the fifth hour (figure 18) differs somewhat from the usual, with stress placed on its center by means of an intersection of registers. The region represented by this hour embodies the West, and it includes all the essential elements of the realm of the dead, including (though it is invisible) the primeval water containing those who have drowned. The hillock with two birds, who are Isis and Nephthys in mourning, is the tumulus over the grave of Osiris, out of which the sun is emerging rejuvenated in the form of a scarab. The "slaughterers" on the far side of the burial mound, along with the various menacing serpents, are entreated to allow the sun god to proceed in peace so that he can get by the narrow pass in the middle of the hour. The four towmen of the fourth hour no longer suffice; here, along with the solar beetle reaching down from above, seven males and seven females pull the towrope. The journey continues through an oval representing the cavern of Sokar, which is nestled between the two heads of the Aker-sphinx (figure 12). This might be yet another representation of the entire netherworld, within which the mysterious nightly union of Osiris (here identified with Sokar) and the sun god takes place. Deeper still, the Lake of Fire is again indicated as a place of punishment.

Quitting the desert of the Land of Sokar, in the sixth hour (figure 19), at the very depths of the netherworld, the sun reaches the water hole filled with Nun, the primeval water. Here lies the corpse of the sun: as a *ba*, the god will unite with it. The sun's corpse is depicted twice, simultaneously, at the ends of the upper and lower registers. It is not depicted as a mummy; rather, it is represented as the solar beetle—the scarab— thus already connected with the god's rejuvenated morning form. The corpse is also the image of Osiris, which is embodied by the leonine "Bull-with-the-thunderous-voice" in the upper register. As *ba* and corpse, Re and Osiris unite at the deepest point in the nocturnal journey, while the notion of resurrection is underscored by the semi-upright position of deities in the upper and lower registers. Only here, at this most critical juncture, are the Kings of Upper and Lower Egypt emphasized, along with the symbols of their might: their scepters, crowns, and uraei. They are here to be present at the resurrection of the deceased pharaoh. Thoth is seated in front of the barque, healing the Eye and thus helping to ignite the new light. The lower register is framed by Sobek and Nun, the

12. Amduat, realm of Sokar in the fifth hour. From the tomb of Tuthmosis III. Photo by
A. Brodbeck.

lords of the primeval waters, while Tatenen, lord of the depths of the
earth, is also mentioned in the texts.

At about midnight, the sun shines anew, but this self-engendering of
Light also represents a moment of grave danger. This is why we find, in
the foreground of the seventh hour (figures 13 and 20), the punishment
of enemies, above all the archfiend Apophis: in the form of a serpent, he
lies on his sand bank in front of the barque, trying to bring the course of
the renewed Light to a standstill. He cannot succeed in this, for he is en-
sorcelled by Isis and Seth, while Selket casts her fetters around his body,
which is dismembered by yet other assistants. Moreover, the sun is now
also protected by the *Mehen*-serpent. Analogously, in the upper register,
Osiris triumphs over his enemies, who have been bound and beheaded
by an avenging demon with a cat's head; Osiris, too, is in the coils of a
protective *Mehen*-serpent. At the end of the upper register, we also see
three divine *ba*-birds with crowned human heads, along with Atum on a
serpent, while behind the sand bank in the middle register, we once
again observe the burial place of the sun's corpse, protected by knives.

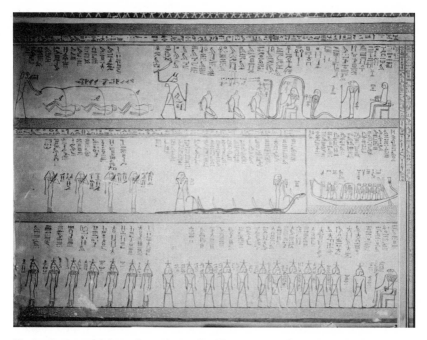

13. Amduat, seventh hour. From the tomb of Tuthmosis III. Photo by A. Brodbeck.

In the lower register, the sun god is enthroned as "Horus of the netherworld," providing for the course of the stars, whose personifications fill the remainder of the register. The conclusion depicts a helpful crocodile with the head of Osiris; it is assisting in the search for those parts of the god's corpse that are drifting in the water.

The well-ordered format of the eighth hour (figure 21) is striking. The upper and lower registers are each divided into five caverns or crypts sealed by doors that open at the bidding of the sun god, as has already taken place in the representation. Nearly all the beings in these crypts are seated on hieroglyphs for cloth, which the caption designates as their clothing. The theme of this hour is thus the supplying of clothes, which from early times on represented a high priority among the things wished for in the afterlife. The texts also describe how the *ba*-souls of the gods and the dead joyfully respond to the sun god from these crypts, which stand for all the crypts in the netherworld. Though the sound of this rejoicing is intelligible speech to the god, human ears hear it only as the cries of animals or other sounds in nature, such as banging on metal or splashing water: such is the distortion even of sound in the afterlife! In the middle register, the solar barque is again towed vigorously along, here by eight males, toward its ultimate destination. Personified *shemes* hieroglyphs appear next, designating both the jurisdiction and the "following" of the god, as well as the four rams of Tatenen, which at the end of the New Kingdom were condensed into the figure of a four-headed solar ram..

The crew of the solar barque is highlighted in the ninth hour (figure 22); with their rudders in their hands, they are the dominating theme of the middle register, where three divine figures concerned with the material provisioning of the dead are also depicted. Additionally, the upper and lower registers continue the eighth hour's theme of providing clothes. At the top, the first group, with their hieroglyphs for cloth, is described as a court of law that "fells the enemies of Osiris," while the following group of goddesses care for Osiris, which includes the repelling of his enemies. The twelve uraei in the lower register also serve as a deterrent to enemies, and the nine "field-gods" who follow, stalks of grain in hand, again assure the provisioning of the deceased.

In the lower register of the tenth hour of the night (figure 23) is the rectangle of water containing those who have drowned, which fills the middle register of the ninth hour in the Book of Gates. Those shown in various positions, drifting in the water like Osiris, are saved from decay and decomposition by Horus, who leads them to a blessed posthumous existence even though they have not been accorded a proper burial. Here, the primeval water reveals itself to be a regenerating element, filling this entire hour of the night, which is designated "(the one) with deep water and high banks." Darkness rules here, moreover, and the hour is lit by the four goddesses with serpents on their heads who are standing behind the watery rectangle. The upper register is devoted to the rescue and healing of the Eye, which appears as the solar Eye and the Eye of Horus. Thoth (the seated baboon) is responsible for this, along with the lion-headed Sakhmet, goddess of healing, who manifests herself here in various forms, while the remaining deities lend extra protection to the Eye. In the middle register, the *ba*-souls of Sokar (the falcon in the serpent) and Osiris (the falcon-headed serpent) make an appearance in front of the solar barque, along with the sun god's bodyguards, who are armed with various weapons to protect him against his enemies in the darkness.

The eleventh hour (figure 24) is filled with preparations for the coming sunrise, the sun's emergence from the eastern mountain of the sky.

"World-encircler," the serpent within which the miracle of the sun's re-juvenation will occur in the next hour, is already present in front of the barque. In the form of serpents, Isis and Nephthys transport the crowns of the Two Lands to the eastern gate of Sais, where four forms of the goddess Neith are standing. In the upper register, the concern is once again with time and the birth of the hours: everything depends on not missing the right moment for the new sunrise. At the end of the upper register, next to the retinue of the sun god, four additional goddesses sit on double serpents, each holding a hand in front of her face; from them emanates the fiery breath that incinerates the enemies who are cast into flame-filled pits in the lower register. The serpent "who burns millions," along with avenging goddesses holding knives, carry out this Last Judg-ment, averting any threat to the rising of the sun. Horus, who is watch-ing over the scene, condemns the enemies of his father.

The rebirth of the sun occurs in the twelfth hour (figure 25). Since it entails a repetition of the original creation, the primeval gods are pres-ent; two pairs of them are represented at the beginning of the lower reg-ister. The sequence of events is situated inside "World-encircler," the serpent that appeared in the eleventh hour, and the gravity of the event is indicated by the unusually large number of figures, twelve males and thirteen females, who are hauling the boat with its "millions" of blessed dead through the body of the gigantic serpent. The backward direction, from tail to mouth, indicates the necessary reversal of time: according to the caption, all these beings enter the serpent's tail old and frail, weak-ened by age, and emerge from its mouth as newborn babes. At the end of the hour, the solar beetle, which was already present in the bow of the barque, flies into the outstretched arms of the god Shu, who will elevate the sun into the daytime sky. The event is accompanied by general re-joicing on the part of the deities in the upper and lower registers, a re-joicing not only for the sun, but also for Osiris, to whom life is promised though he must remain in the realm of the dead. Additionally, the god-desses in the upper register drive off Apophis one last time by means of fire-spitting snakes, with the support of the oarsmen in the lower regis-ter, who accompany the sun in safety to the sky. When the sun has left the netherworld, the goddesses will continue to provide the dead with the light from their living torches. For a moment, the netherworld lies open, but Shu seals it again, and the nocturnal journey is over. Along with Osiris, who is depicted mummiform at the end of the lower regis-ter, all the deceased sink back into the sleep of death.

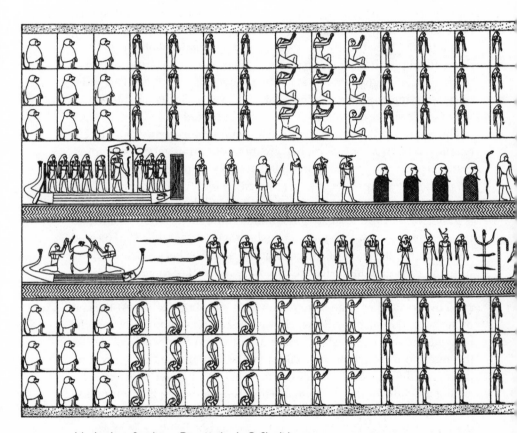

14. Amduat, first hour. Drawing by A. G. Shedid.

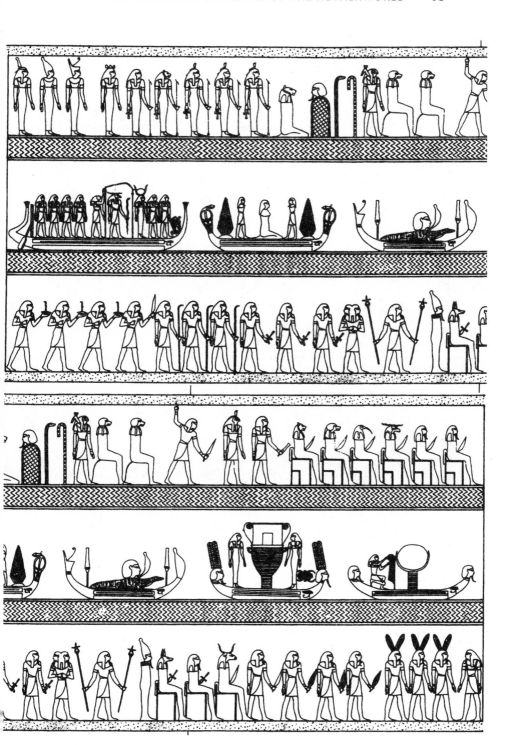

15. Amduat, second hour. Drawing by A. G. Shedid.

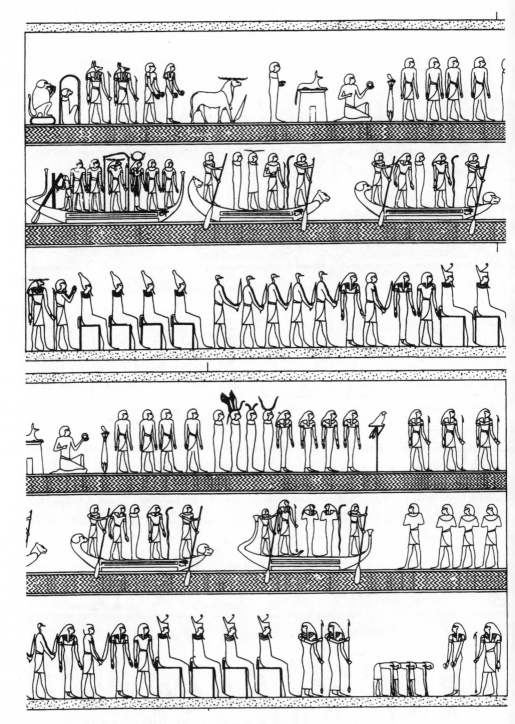

16. Amduat, third hour. Drawing by A. G. Shedid.

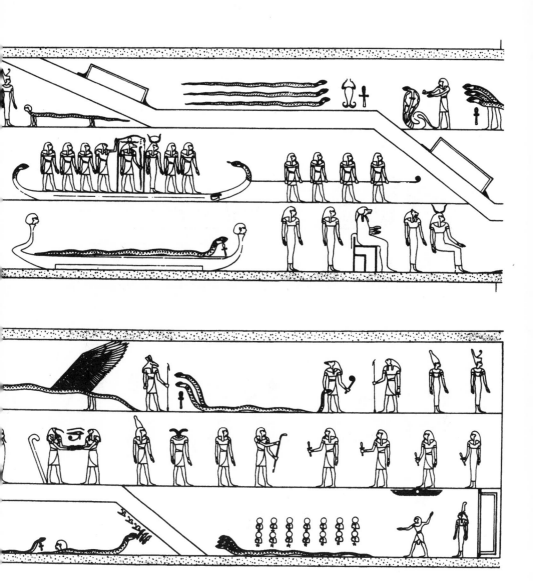

17. Amduat, fourth hour. Drawing by A. G. Shedid.

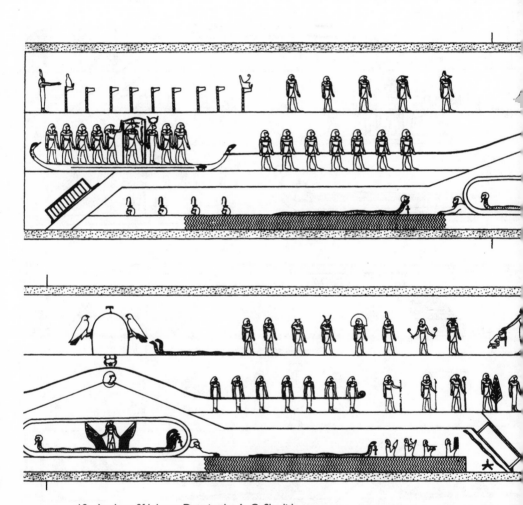

18. Amduat, fifth hour. Drawing by A. G. Shedid.

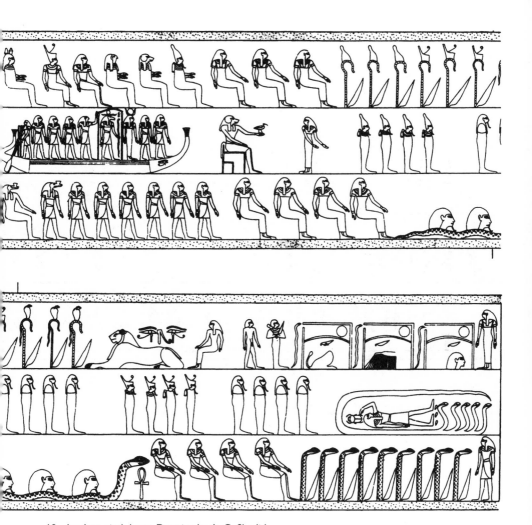

19. Amduat, sixth hour. Drawing by A. G. Shedid.

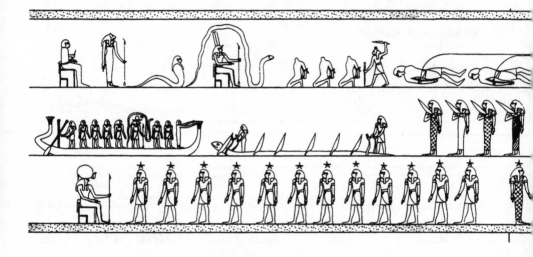

20. Amduat, seventh hour. Drawing by A. G. Shedid.

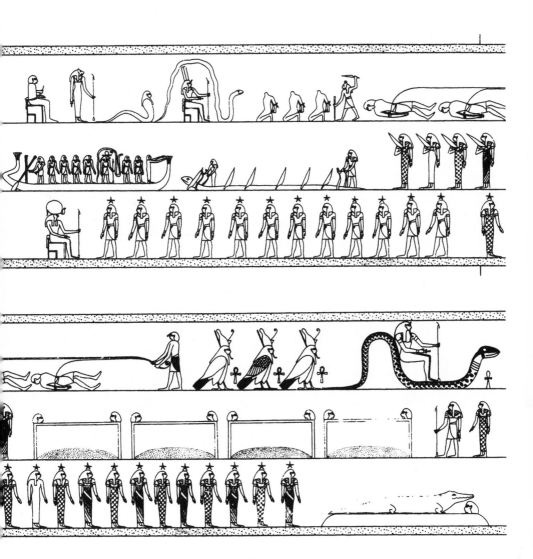

21. Amduat, eighth hour. Drawing by A. G. Shedid.

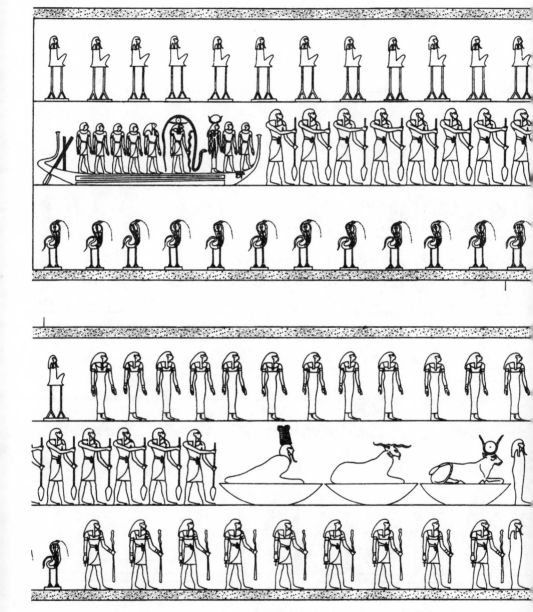

22. Amduat, ninth hour. Drawing by A. G. Shedid.

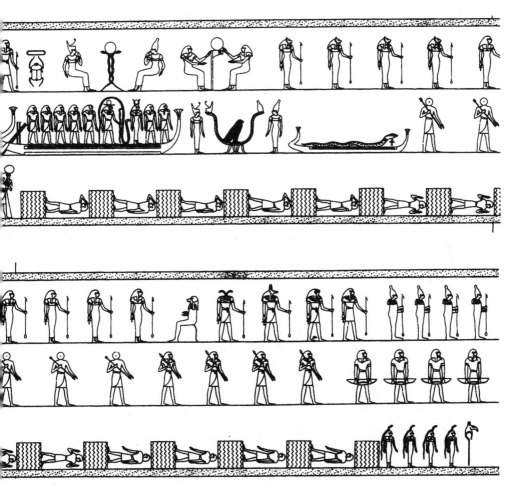

23. Amduat, tenth hour. Drawing by A. G. Shedid.

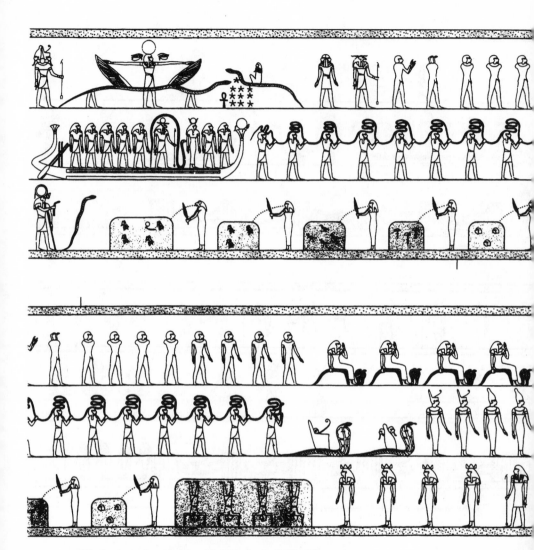

24. Amduat, eleventh hour. Drawing by A. G. Shedid.

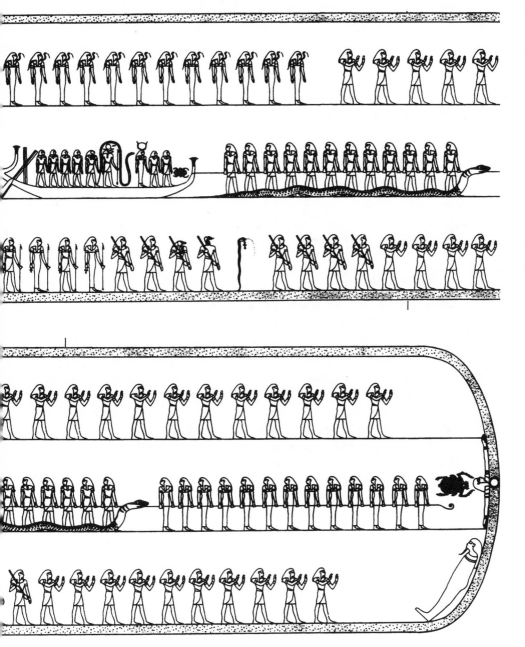

25. Amduat, twelfth hour. Drawing by A. G. Shedid.

26. Spell of the Twelve Caves. After Edouard Naville, *Das Ägyptische Todtenbuch der XVIII. bis XX. Dynastie*, vol. I (Berlin, 1886), plate CLXXXVII.

The Spell of the Twelve Caves

The illustrated text of The Spell of the Twelve Caves (figure 26) is first attested on a papyrus (Cairo CG 24742) from the tomb of Amenophis II. Merneptah had a second royal version inserted in the southern chamber of the Osireion at Abydos. Since the texts and representation also occur in Books of the Dead from Dynasty 18 on, it has been considered spell 168 of this work since the edition of Naville; Alexandre Piankoff first recognized it as a composition in and of itself. With its description of the twelve caves (*qereret* in Egyptian) of the netherworld and their divine inhabitants, it is related to the Books of the Netherworld, especially the older type in which the netherworld is divided into twelve sections representing hours. A title for the composition, "spell for allowing Osiris NN to enter," is found only on Papyrus BM 10478. The textual tradition reaches down to the threshold of the Ptolemaic Period; the tomb of Petosiris has a scene from the ninth cavern, and traces are found in the early Ptolemaic Book of Hours edited by Raymond O. Faulkner.

Each cave contains a variable number of groups of deities; thus, the eighth has seven and the ninth a maximum of twenty groups. The first seven caves are included only in the Osireion, though the inhabitants there are represented quite schematically—alternately as three mummies or three anthropomorphic deities, in each case two male and one female. Thus, only the eighth through the twelfth caves are portrayed in detail. It is striking that inimical beings and scenes of punishment are completely absent. The division into caves does not occur in some manuscripts, with the groups of deities instead represented sequentially.

While the Osireion depicts the deities of each group in their entirety, the remaining versions show only a single male or female representative and add the relevant number. In the case of Amenophis II, these numerals, as in his offering lists, are written in a separate strip underneath the figures, whereas on other papyri they are immediately next to them; on some papyri, the numbers are lacking. The number four is predominant, but the numbers one, two, eight, nine, thirteen, fourteen, and thirty-one occur, while three seems to be entirely absent.

Under the strip containing the representations of the deities, their names, and their number, a register of text contains a notation regarding each group's offerings on earth, which is comparable to the Book of Gates. In the Osireion, the king is shown kneeling in front of each group, making offerings. Papyrus BM 10478 and later papyri frame the strips of depictions in the middle with two registers of texts; the upper one indicates, next to the names of the deities, the beneficent deeds they perform for the deceased. Additionally, the papyrus in the British Museum places the entire composition within a shrine.

The deities grant various favors to the deceased. For instance, Re grants the ability to see when he rises; free movement in the realm of the dead and free passage through the gates of the netherworld; light in the midst of its darkness; food, drink, and protection of all sorts; and vindication against all enemies.

The Book of Gates
Sources

According to Hartwig Altenmüller, the Book of Gates belongs to "the period before the New Kingdom" because of its similarity to the Amduat, but the cosmopolitan spirit of the scene containing foreigners speaks against this. Other indications point instead to the Amarna Period as its date of origin. In the tomb of Haremhab, the earliest, albeit incomplete, exemplar of the book was placed in the sarcophagus chamber, where until then the Amduat had been customary. Ramesses I also employed this book alone, while Sethos I decorated his sarcophagus chamber with the Amduat while reserving the Book of Gates for his two great pillared halls (E and J); though he used only the first half of the book on the walls of these halls, his alabaster sarcophagus is decorated with the earliest complete and continuous version. Ramesses II and his successors also employed the book in their upper pillared halls, sarcophagus chambers, and subsidiary rooms, while Merneptah decorated the right wall of the corridor of the cenotaph of Sethos I at Abydos with a complete Book of Gates, complemented by the Book of Caverns on the left wall. In his tomb and in those of his successors down through Ramesses IV, it dominated the walls of the sarcophagus chamber; Ramesses VI was the first king to choose a new solution, the Book of the Earth, though a complete Book of Gates was included in the upper portion of his tomb. Ramesses VII was the last pharaoh to use portions of the book (the first and second hours) in the single corridor of his tomb; under Ramesses IX it disappeared from the royal tomb, though the gates guarded by serpents represented at the beginnings of the corridors (as also in the tomb of Prince Mentuhirkhopshef, KV 19) are a last echo of the composition. The book also appears on royal sarcophagi, though only in selection; thus, the sarcophagus of Ramesses III has only the first hour. Tjanefer, a priest of Amun under Ramesses III, was allowed to use a selection of scenes from the book in his tomb (TT 158).

Following the end of the New Kingdom, portions of the book were used only sporadically, perhaps because it is oriented more thoroughly than the Amduat to the person of the king. The Book of the Dead of Anhai, which may date to Dynasty 20, and the mythological papyrus of Khonsumes of Dynasty 21 contain the concluding representation from the book, as does the Dynasty 26 tomb of Mutirdis; other extracts are found in the tombs of Petamenophis at Thebes and Horiraa at Saqqara from this same period. The first hour and the judgment hall occur often on late sarcophagi, and, in one instance (CG 29306), the twenty-first scene is depicted.

Research

The scene containing foreigners in the tomb of Sethos I and the Judgment of the Dead in that of Ramesses VI aroused the interest of visitors at an early date, and they were often copied. Jean-François Champollion provided the first description, along with translations from the book, in his thirteenth letter from Egypt, dated May 26, 1829; relying for the most part on the tomb of Ramesses VI, he supposed that the Book of Gates described the daytime journey of the sun while the Book of Caverns on the opposite wall described its nocturnal journey. From 1864 on, the highly reliable publication of the alabaster sarcophagus of Sethos I by Bonomi and Sharpe served as the basic text edition. Gaston Maspero coined the designation *Livre de Portes* ("Book of Gates," along with *Livre des Pylônes*, "Book of the Pylons"; Eugène Lefébure called it *Livre de l'Enfer*, "Book of the Netherworld") and supplied a brief survey of its contents in an essay in 1888, after Lefébure had already published the first translation of the text on the alabaster sarcophagus in 1878 and 1881. Budge described and translated the version on the sarcophagus in 1905 and compared its hours of the night with those in the Amduat; but because the lid had been destroyed from the sixth hour on, he arrived at a false enumeration. The Osireion with its complete version had been discovered in 1902, and in 1908, the earliest, though incomplete, version was found in the tomb of Haremhab; the latter was published as early as 1912. Next, Charles Maystre and Alexandre Piankoff created a broader textual basis with their text edition of 1939–1962, which was replaced by that of Erik Hornung in 1979. Piankoff's complete English translation has been available since 1954 and Hornung's complete German translation since 1972.

Structure and Language

An original title is not attested. Although the structure of the book is quite similar to that of the Amduat, with twelve nocturnal hours each divided into three registers, it differs from it by means of the gates depicted at the end of each hour. Another clear difference is in the solar barque, where only two other gods, Sia and Heka, are depicted along with the sun god as opposed to the numerous crew in the Amduat. Here, the cabin of the boat is surrounded in each hour by a protective *Mehen*-serpent, and in each hour, four male figures are depicted like hieroglyphs towing the barque; in the sarcophagus chambers of Haremhab, Ramesses I, and Sethos I, their clothing and beards clearly mark them as human rather than divine beings, and thus as deceased persons. Long concluding texts are absent; instead, in the middle and at the end, depictions of the Judgment of the Dead and the course of the sun are emphasized by their not being divided into registers. The first hour of the night occupies a special position, as in the Amduat, and its structure differs from that of the other hours. The last three hours also display unusual features in that they omit the main figure (Atum or Horus) in the lower register and depict only deities and not the blessed dead. The gates of these last three hours, as well as the one in front of the hall of judgment, also display peculiarities.

In no other Book of the Netherworld do the gates of the hereafter appear as visibly and systematically as here. It is most easily compared with the gates of Book of the Dead spells 144 and 145 (with variants), which Egyptians of the Ramesside Period considered a "substitute" for the Book of Gates in nonroyal tombs such as that of Nefertari and others in the Valley of the Queens, or in the case of Twosre in the Valley of the Kings (in the front part of the tomb); the tomb of Tjanefer (TT 158) displays a unique mixture in that the solar barque, rather than the deceased, appears in front of the gates. Some confusion still arises from the designation of Book of the Dead spells that contain gates as the Book of Gates, as in the bibliography of Porter and Moss; we must draw a clear distinction, for gates in the afterlife are found as early as the Pyramid Texts. The twelve gates of the netherworld are already presupposed in the text of the Amduat, though they are not yet represented there. Their designation *sebekhet* corresponds to that employed in BD 145, although the latter amount to twenty-one. In BD 144, there are seven gates, called *areret*. In the Book of Gates, each gate has a guardian in the form of a serpent on its door, as well as two further guardians with menacing names and fire-spitting uraei.

Although more deities and deceased persons are depicted than in the Amduat—more than a thousand, in fact—they are more regularly combined into groups, and they bear fewer individual names, with the result that their number is easier to keep track of. Many of these groups are not intended as deities but rather as deceased persons. In contrast to the Amduat, notations concerning the use of the Book are absent. Instead, there are remarks about offerings, which as a rule are located at the end of a scene, though such remarks are lacking in scenes depicting enemies and in the final three hours. Of the total of one hundred scenes, many fill an entire register, though the last two hours contain a number of brief individual scenes. The Middle Egyptian of the texts displays scarcely any influences from Late Egyptian. In his *Komparative Untersuchungen zu vier Unterweltsbüchern*, Winfried Barta established that the Book of Gates has an especially rich vocabulary (see the bibliography under "New Kingdom Books of the Netherworld, General").

The judgment hall of Osiris occupies a special, central position. Provided with texts in cryptographic writing, it is inserted into the fifth gateway so that it is situated immediately before the union with the sun's corpse in the sixth hour. Beginning with the tomb of Sethos I, it is replaced by a scene depicting the king before the enthroned (later, standing) Osiris, thus depicting no longer the judgment but rather the identification of Pharaoh with the ruler of the dead. For the first time, a separate concluding representation summarizes the entire course of the sun in a single scene; at the same time, similar scenes appear as illustrations to the solar hymns of the Book of the Dead (spell 16).

On the sarcophagus of Sethos I, the hours are in a continuous sequence, beginning with the outside of the foot end and ending with the inside of the head end, so that the concluding scene occurs directly behind the head of the deceased. The Osireion and the tomb of Ramesses VI also display a continuous arrangement, whereas in the remaining tombs, the hours are distributed over various walls and rooms; from Sethos I to Ramesses III, the upper pillared hall was preferred for the fifth and sixth hours of the night.

Content

As in the case of the Amduat, the composition is concerned with the nocturnal journey of the sun. In part, the contents of the hours are displaced just a bit from where they occur in the Amduat: thus, the drowned appear in the ninth hour rather than in the tenth. Deities and the blessed dead are more clearly distinguished from one another than they are in the Amduat, and the dead seem bound to their respective regions in the hours of the night. The special status of Pharaoh is more evident, for he accompanies the sun god to his rebirth in the morning, thus reflecting the course of the sun in his journey through the netherworld. In most versions, various additions to the texts and representations refer directly to the king.

Upon his entry into the realm of the dead (figure 30), the sun god is greeted not by individual deities but by the collective of the dead, who are designated the "gods of the west" and located in the western mountain range. As in the Amduat, the first hour of the night is an interstitial realm preceding the actual netherworld, which begins at the first gate. Two stakes, one bearing a ram's head and the other a jackal's, embody the commanding power of the god, which both rewards and punishes those who dwell in the hereafter.

The second hour (figures 27 and 31) makes a clear distinction between the blessed dead in the upper register, who have spoken Maat and now live on Maat, and the damned in the lower register, who are reprimanded by Atum. In the middle register, the barque encounters the "gods in the entrance," while in the lower register, the four Weary Ones are represented along with the "enemies," indicating that here, even the cardinal points are exhausted and need to be lifted up.

The third hour (figures 28 and 32) highlights certain central motifs of the nightly journey, such as the mummies in the upper register, which

27. Book of Gates, second hour: Atum and the Weary Ones. From the tomb of Sethos I. Photo by A. Brodbeck.

are awakened from the dead and animated in their shrines, and the ambivalent Lake of Fire, from which the blessed dead are provisioned but whose waters are flames for the damned. In the middle register, the sun god is towed along in the "barque of the earth," a symbolic condensation of his entire journey through the depths of the earth. Also symbolic of renewal is the outfitting with sparkling white linen indicated at the end of the register. In the lower register, Apophis makes his first appearance, here as a giant serpent in front of Atum, who is assisted by two Enneads in overcoming this archfiend.

Two bodies of water dominate the upper register of the fourth hour (figure 33): the Lake of Life, which is guarded by jackals, and the Lake of Uraei; both are perhaps variations on the Lake of Fire in the third hour. In front of the barque in the middle register lie shrines containing mummies still in the sleep of death; the sun god effects their resurrection and provisioning. Their renewed life in the hereafter occupies an entire hour of the night. The passing of the hours is laid out in the following scene, with its many-coiled serpent representing time and its twelve goddesses

28. Book of Gates, beginning of the third hour. From the tomb of Ramesses IV. Photo by A. Brodbeck.

embodying the hours. In the lower register, the enshrined Osiris is surrounded protectively on all sides by the gods of his entourage. As a
loyal son, Horus cares for his deceased father, while the enemies of the
god are being punished in the fiery pits at the end of the register.

The contents of the fifth hour of the night (figure 34) are rather complex. Here, the deceased are allotted space (in the form of fields; therefore
the gods are depicted with a surveying cord in the upper register) and
time (the gods carrying the body of a serpent and the hieroglyphs meaning "lifetime" in the lower register). So that this can occur unhindered,
the archfiend Apophis, the "Retreater" in front of the barque, must once
again be fettered and held fast. Behind him, we see the *ba*-souls of the
blessed dead, and at the beginning of the lower register appear the four
"races" of humankind—Egyptians, Asiatics, Nubians, and Libyans—
each represented by four individuals; existence in the hereafter is assured
to all of them, and they are placed in the care of Horus and Sakhmet. Just
as in the Great Hymn of Akhenaten the Aten is said to care even for for-
eign peoples, so here they are sheltered in the realm of the dead.

The portrayal of the judgment hall is emphasized by its insertion as a
special scene (figure 29) immediately before the sixth hour; it is the only
depiction of the Judgment of the Dead in the Books of the Netherworld,
and it is also distinguished by the use of cryptographic writing. As judge,
Osiris sits enthroned on a stepped dais while the personified scale in front
of him, unlike that in the Book of the Dead, displays empty pans. An Ennead of blessed, justified dead stand on the steps, and the enemies lying
invisibly under their feet are consigned to the Place of Annihilation. Yet
another inimical power is being driven off, this time in the form of a pig.

The Judgment of the Dead here is thus the prelude to the union of the
ba and the corpse of the sun god (like those of all the blessed deceased)
in the sixth hour of the night (figure 35), which lies at the deepest point
in the journey. As in the Amduat, the corpse of the sun is in the middle
register, though here it remains invisible; immediately in front of the
barque and its towmen, it is being carried by gods whose arms are
equally invisible, hidden because of their contact with the corpse. In the
register below, mummies of deceased persons are lying on a long,
serpent-shaped bed in order to participate in the union with the *ba* and
the resurrection effected by it. So that this critical event is not interfered
with, the archfiend Apophis must be kept at a distance, a feat being ac-
complished by the gods holding forked poles in the upper register; from
the serpent's body rise the heads of people Apophis has swallowed and
is now obliged to set free again. In the immediate vicinity is a representation of time as a twisted double rope that is being unwound from the

29. Book of Gates, judgment hall of Osiris. From the tomb of Haremhab. Photo by F. Teichmann.

pharynx of the god Aqen. The lower register ends with a depiction of
the Lake of Fire, which this time is circular and inhabited by a cobra that
serves as an effective deterrent to all enemies.

As in the Amduat, the central theme of the seventh hour (figure 36) is
the elimination of any and all inimical powers, so that the sun's renewal
will not be endangered. In front of the solar barque in the middle register appear the jackal-headed "stakes of Geb," with two enemies of the
god bound to each of them; punishing demons with ominous names see
to their torment, to which Re consents. In sharp contrast to this scene,
the upper register depicts two groups of blessed dead, one with baskets
filled with grain as a sign of their material provisioning and the other
with the feather of Maat as a symbol of their vindication in the Judgment of the Dead. They all have "existence until its end," sheltered in
Maat, while the condemned belong to the Place of Annihilation. In the
caption, Osiris welcomes his new followers. In the lower register, deities
or deceased people busy themselves with huge ears of grain intended
for their assured provisions, or are provided with sickles for harvesting
them; under the rays of the revived sun, even grain can grow in abundance here.

The eighth hour (figure 37) once again includes a depiction of time as an endless rope spooled out hour by hour, as in the sixth hour, and also as the towrope of the barque, which "produces mysteries." In front of the barque in the middle register are the "lords of provision in the west," whom Re commissions to allocate provisions to the blessed and inflict evil on the enemies. The mummies in the lower register have turned over on their biers and are thus in the process of resurrection. Next to them, a council of judges provides protection.

In the ninth hour (figure 38), the central motif in front of the barque in the middle register is the rectangle of water containing the drowned, a scene borrowed from the Amduat, where it is depicted in the lower register of the tenth hour. Here, four groups of dead persons drift in various positions in the primeval waters of Nun, profiting from its regenerative capacities; for them, the water means refreshment. Their noses are to breathe the air, and their *ba*-souls will not be destroyed, with the result that they will share in the continued existence of the blessed. Re himself is here the "one who is in Nun," and in the scene that concludes the book, he will be raised up out of Nun. The aforementioned *ba*-souls appear in the upper register, and next to them is a group of persons who give them bread and vegetables. By way of contrast, the lower register is reserved for punishment. The Fiery One, a giant serpent with the Children of Horus standing in his coils, spews his fiery breath at twelve enemies who are bound in three different ways. In his reprimand, Horus condemns these enemies for the atrocities they have committed against his father, Osiris, and he summons the Fiery One to set them ablaze.

In the tenth hour (figure 39), the entire middle register is filled with the battle against Apophis. The fourteen deities holding nets are especially striking. In their nets, which they hold above them, magical power is contained as though in a force field, and it renders Apophis defenseless. The Old One (perhaps the earth god, Geb) ties fetters around his body. The upper and lower registers display special forms of manifestation of the sun god. Above, he appears as a griffin, followed by two highly complex serpent entities who participate in the punishment of Apophis and all other enemies. In the lower register, a continuous rope connects all the figures; the sun god is depicted in the center as a falcon, though he is also called Khepri ("scarab beetle"). The accompanying text mentions "emergence" and stresses that the journey is proceeding toward the sky.

Again in the eleventh hour (figure 40), this time in the upper register, Apophis is bound, dismembered, and rendered harmless. The rope with which he and his assistants are bound is held by a giant fist emerging from the depths. In the middle register, the face of Re is making its way in a barque, so that the dead can gaze upon the countenance of the god. The reversed direction of the barque is striking; could this be an allusion to the reversal of time, as in the twelfth hour of the Amduat (see page 41)? The god is preceded by stars that herald his reappearance. In the lower register, the oarsmen of the god make their appearance, together with the goddesses of the hours; time and energy (rowing) collaborate to propel the barque up into the eastern horizon. Several deities are already performing the function of announcing the god in the horizon; their cry is a presentiment of the din that will accompany the rising of the sun (as at the beginning of Goethe's *Faust*, part II: "What an uproar the light brings!").

The sun god arrives at the twelfth and last hour of the night (figure 41), in which the miracle of his rebirth will occur, through the gate "with the mysterious entrance." The mystery of sunrise, into which the dead are here inducted, unfolds in several individual scenes, beginning in the upper register with gods who "carry the blazing light," which is represented concretely by the sun disks in their hands. Stars again prefigure the appearance of the sun, while goddesses seated atop serpents surround the solar child. Even here, his barque remains unchanged. In front of it lies Apophis, already in fetters; the fiend is unable to impede the sunrise, and he is held in check by gods wielding knives and shepherds' crooks. Behind him, four baboons announce the sun god in the eastern horizon, their hands in a gesture of jubilation. The lower register is concerned with crowns as symbols of power that are to be worn while leaving the netherworld, as well as with the upbringing of the already newborn sun by his "nurses" and with mourning for Osiris, who is to remain behind in the netherworld. In the form of uraei, Isis and Nephthys guard the final gate of the netherworld, through which the sun god will make his entrance onto the horizon.

The concluding representation that follows lacks the usual division into registers. Here, the entire course of the sun is condensed into a single picture, as was the case after the Amarna Period in innumerable illustrations accompanying solar hymns. Half hidden in its depths, the god Nun raises the solar barque out of the primeval waters, which are indicated by wavy lines. In the barque, the sun, in the form of a soaring scarab beetle, is embraced by Isis and Nephthys, while the beetle pushes the sun disk toward the sky goddess Nut, who receives the god Re. Her upside-down position designates the inversion of the sun's course, which will now once again run in the opposite direction from its course through the netherworld, here embodied by Osiris, who surrounds the netherworld with his curved body. All three of the interior spaces of the cosmos are thus contained in this complex representation: the primeval waters, the height of the heavens, and the depths of the earth (the netherworld). From above and below, arms are stretched toward the sun, arms that hold it and move it through these cosmic spaces, day after day.

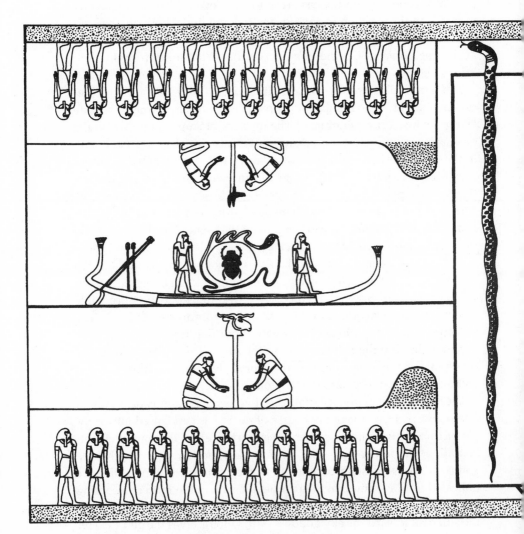

30. Book of Gates, first hour. Drawing by A. G. Shedid.

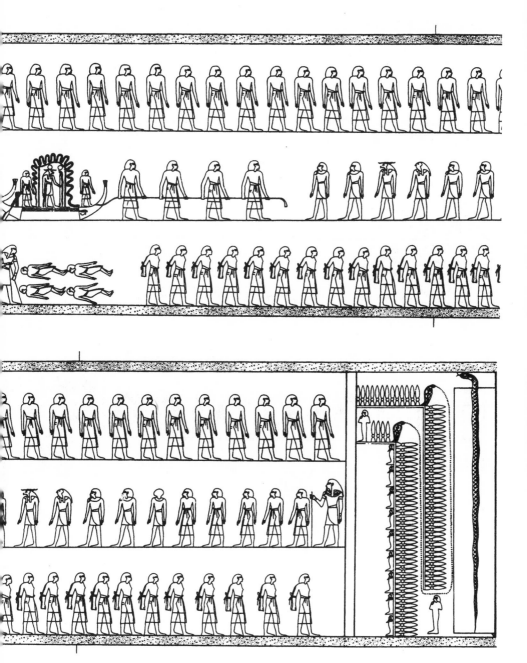

31. Book of Gates, second hour. Drawing by A. G. Shedid.

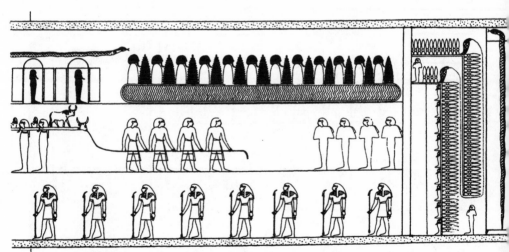

32. Book of Gates, third hour. Drawing by A. G. Shedid.

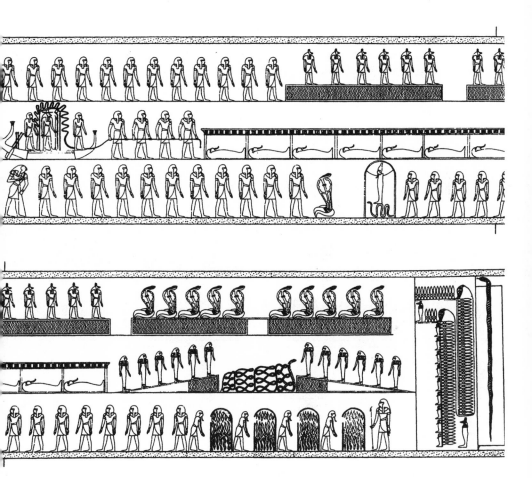

33. Book of Gates, fourth hour. Drawing by A. G. Shedid.

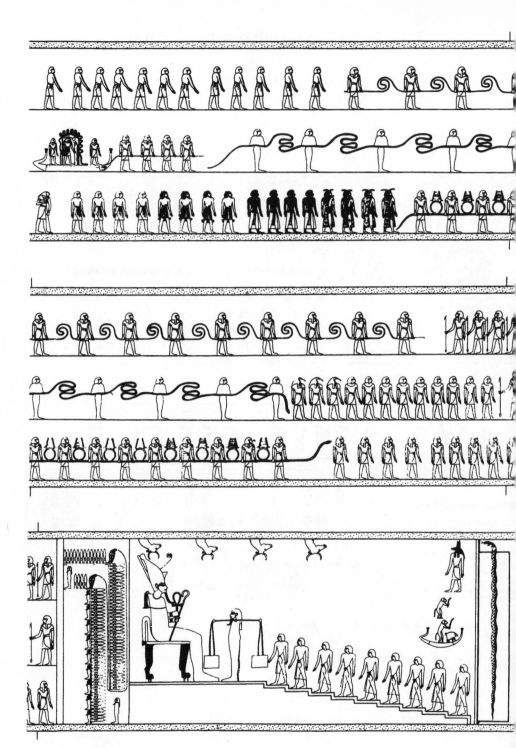

34. Book of Gates, fifth hour. Drawing by A. G. Shedid.

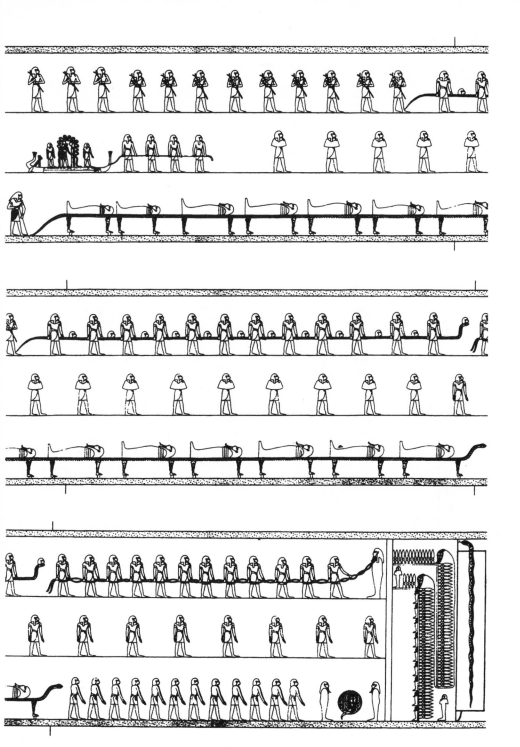

35. Book of Gates, sixth hour. Drawing by A. G. Shedid.

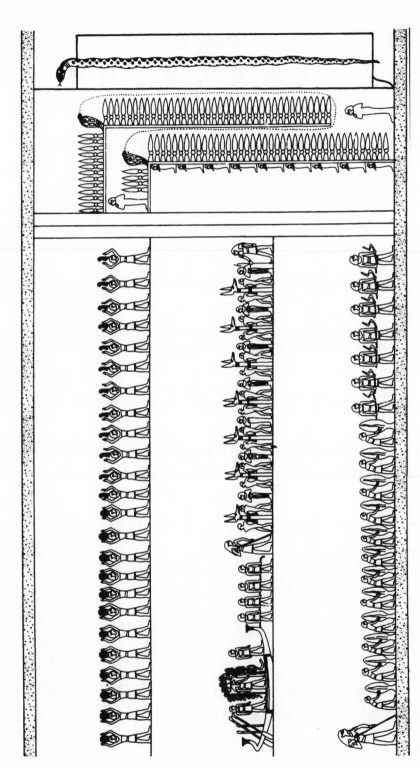

36. Book of Gates, seventh hour. Drawing by A. G. Shedid.

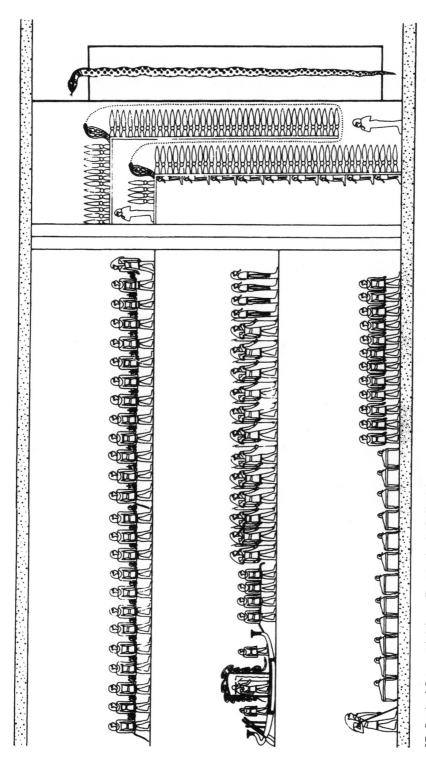

37. Book of Gates, eighth hour. Drawing by A. G. Shedid.

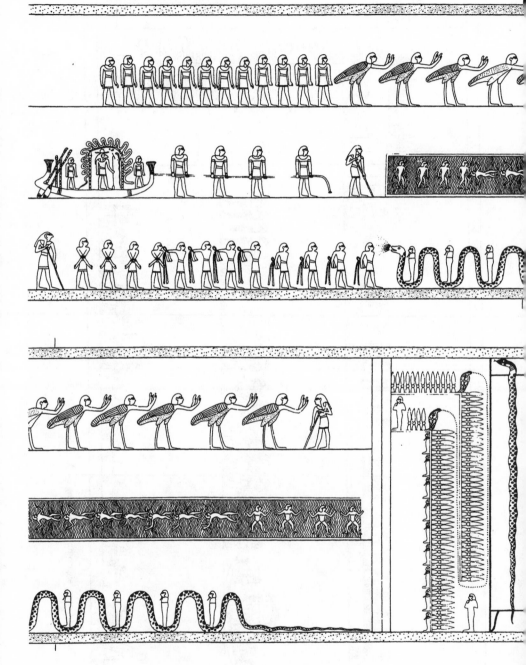

38. Book of Gates, ninth hour. Drawing by A. G. Shedid.

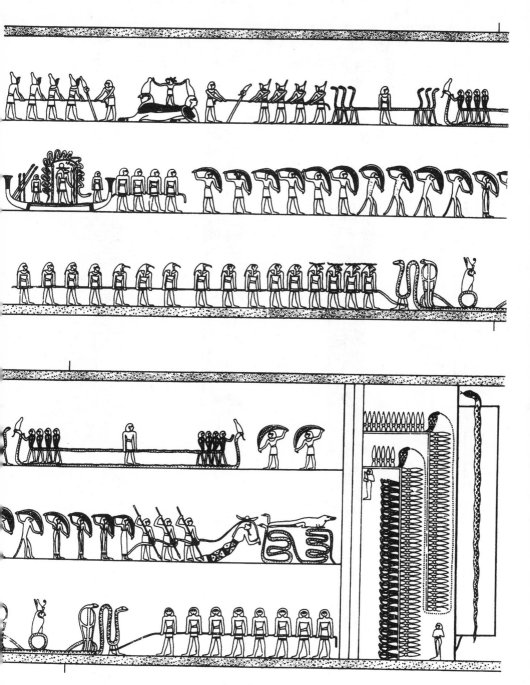

39. Book of Gates, tenth hour. Drawing by A. G. Shedid.

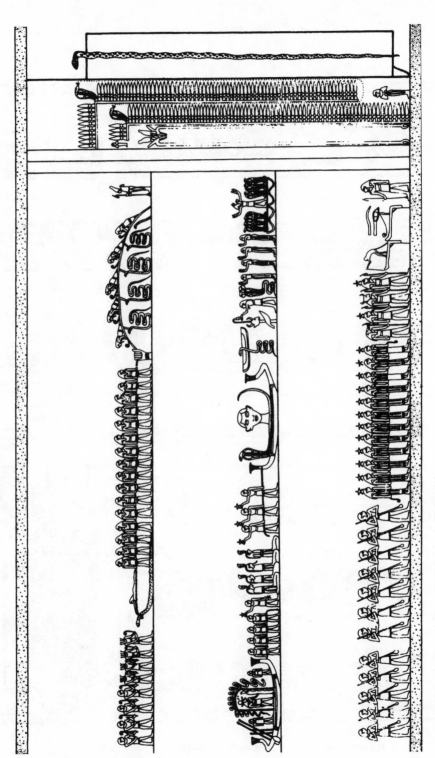

40. Book of Gates, eleventh hour. Drawing by A. G. Shedid.

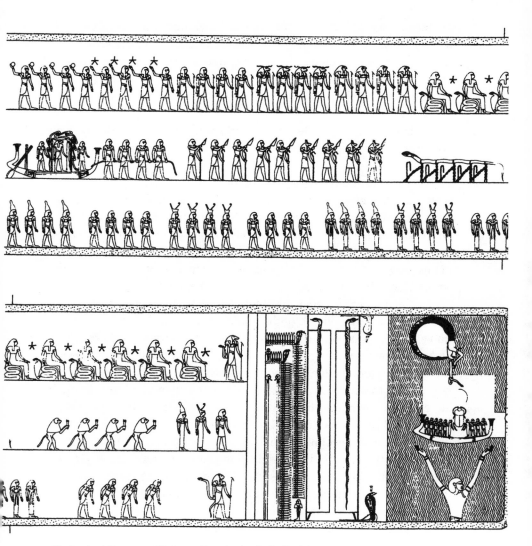

41. Book of Gates, twelfth hour. Drawing by A. G. Shedid.

The Enigmatic Book of the Netherworld

The second gilded shrine of Tutankhamun, counting from the outside, displays two sections from a book that has no parallels, though they are clearly analogous to the two scenes from the Amduat that are depicted on the king's third shrine. It remains unclear whether these are complete hours of the night, given that Tutankhamun's hours from the Amduat are incomplete. In a caption, the book is designated as an "Amduat," the term serving for the first time here as the designation of the genre. Like the Amduat, it is divided into three registers, though the solar barque is absent, and, as in the Book of Caverns, the presence of the sun god is indicated by sun disks in section B and by ram-headed *ba*-birds in the sun disks in section A.

The book is not provided with a title, and the modern designation (Winfried Barta uses the term *Kryptograph*) rests on the fact that in both sections, all the texts and names are in enigmatic writing, with no translations into normal hieroglyphs. The normally written portions of text scattered throughout all the registers stem from the Book of the Dead. Such a combination of a Book of the Netherworld and the Book of the Dead is unique to this instance; not until Dynasty 21 were elements from the Amduat and the Book of the Dead occasionally combined, and it remains uncertain whether the spells here are in fact integral parts of the composition. Section A (figure 42), which begins with two boundary posts, presumably precedes the other section, for the boundary posts are also found at the beginning of the Book of Gates, in the first hour. Additionally, light plays a role in section B, whereas darkness and the Place of Annihilation dominate section A. It remains an open question whether the book had any sections beyond these two. Section B is dominated by rays of light that emanate from disks, stars, or serpents and flow through all the entities, while section A displays only two large disks containing ram-headed *ba*s. Piankoff explains this as the "refilling" of the sun disk during the night. Section A is divided at its midpoint by the figure of a huge god that spans the entire height of the three registers; John C. Darnell sees in this a union of Re and Osiris. After the initial representation, with its two posts (the ram-headed "head of Re" and the jackal-headed "neck of Re") and the solar *ba* in its disk, the first two scenes in the upper and lower register each display eight deities; the upper ones are in the "caverns of the Duat (?)" and in darkness, while those below are located in the Place of Annihilation, though their *ba*-souls are able to accompany the sun god. The head and the feet of the huge divine figure are each surrounded by an *ouroboros*-serpent, which in each case is called *Mehen;* this is the earliest known representation of the *ouroboros,* and the entire figure, with its captions, refers to the genesis and the end of time. The motif of the solar *ba* in its disk, which this time is tied to a towrope, is repeated on his body.

The second half of section A contains three scenes, arranged vertically. In the middle register, seven figures with their arms raised in a gesture of praise turn to the solar *ba* and receive the rays of his disk. Above them, turned in the opposite direction, are seven goddesses in their coffins who behold the rays of the sun and follow the sun god with their *ba*-souls, while their bodies remain in place. The lower register, which is flanked by two guardian figures, again refers to the Place of Annihilation, which Re lights up "with his voice," allowing its inhabitants to breathe. A human-headed serpent is coiled several times around two sarcophagi containing the corpses of Osiris and Re; Darnell reads the large oval containing hands as "coffer" (i.e., of Osiris, with the ram once again referring to Re).

Section B (figure 43) has three registers, each with three scenes; the presence of Re is indicated by means of sun disks belonging to each scene and, in part, even to each figure. The disks are for the most part connected to the figures by rays of light, a pictorial reference to statements in the text that the light of Re enters their bodies. The upper and the lower registers each begin with a spitting cobra. Each of the six gods in the first scene of the upper register has a *ba*-bird in front of him and receives light from a star (though the first one receives it directly from the cobra); according to the caption, it is the light of Re, which enters them. The second scene in the upper register begins with a cat. The seven figures who follow have no heads; instead, each has a face depicted frontally before him, in each case inserted between a star and a sun disk with rays. Above them, light pours directly into their bodies from other sun disks with legs. This is evidently a matter of the separation and rejoining of the head and the body. Each of the six gods of the final scene stands on a *Mehen*-serpent, which helps with his regeneration, and receives life-giving light from a disk in front of him.

The middle register of section B begins with a mummy that has turned itself over and now extends a hand to the ram-headed solar *ba*, which the caption also mentions; from the mummy's feet rears a serpent flooded by light. There follow four lion-headed beings whose arms are hidden, perhaps because they are carrying the corpse of the sun, as in the sixth hour of the Book of Gates. The next scene is nearly identical, though there are now six lion-headed beings; in each scene, light from a sun disk atop a pair of legs enters the mouths of all the beings represented there.

In the first scene of the lower register, the cobra at the beginning spits light that in each instance is received by a lion's head and emitted again by a cobra next to it; it pours over six Osiris figures who, according to

the caption, are "clothed" (Darnell's reading) with light by Re while their
ba-souls follow them. That they are also granted breath is shown by the
sail hieroglyphs—signifying "wind" or "breath"—in front of them. The
middle scene begins with a lion; like the cat in the upper register, it is
rising up out of the earth, in which a serpent is hidden. The next six
mummiform figures are ram-headed, and in normal writing, the caption
names the deceased king as the object of their regard. The last scene consists of six goddesses, each of whom receives light from a disk and lets it
pour from her hands onto the head of the serpent named Evil of Face;
their names designate them as punishing beings, though they also carry
the sun, depicted as a star and a disk, in their wombs. Throughout this
section, the intensity of the role played by light in the realm of the dead
is striking; ideas from King Akhenaten's religion of light seem to be still
at work here.

At the end of the section, the sun disk with its ram-headed *ba* appears
once again, now doubled. It is embedded in a symbolic summary of the
daily course of the sun, wherein it is kept in constant motion by four
pairs of arms. Serpents and the heads of four *negau*-cattle, along with
goddesses making the gesture of praise, an Osiris figure, and an "arm of
Re," positioned antithetically, complete the scene. I recognize it as a concluding scene, though Darnell prefers to see it as a beginning, because a
similar representation appears on the ceiling of corridor G in the tomb of
Ramesses VI.

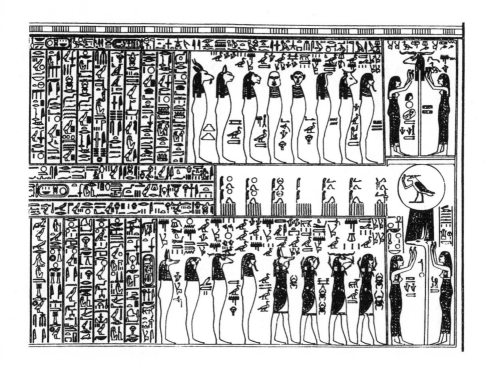

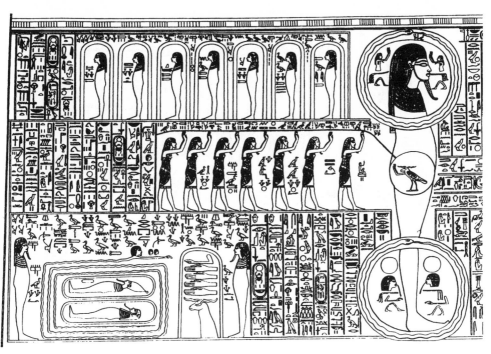

42. Enigmatic Book of the Afterlife, section A. After A. Piankoff, *Les chapelles de Tout-Ankh-Amon* (Cairo, 1951–1952), plate II.

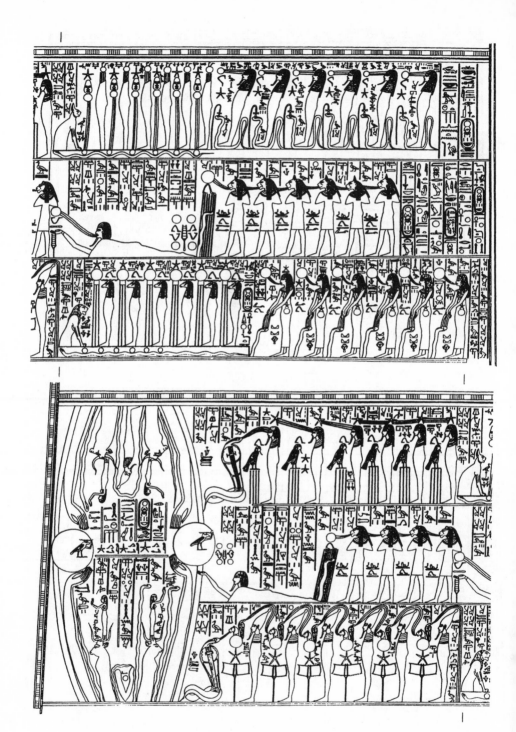

43. Enigmatic Book of the Netherworld, section B. After A. Piankoff, *Les chapelles de Tout-Ankh-Amon* (Cairo, 1951–1952), plate IV.

The Book of Caverns

Sources

The earliest, nearly complete version of The Book of Caverns—its upper register is now partially destroyed—appeared in the Osireion (the cenotaph of Sethos I) at Abydos under Merneptah; it occupies the left wall of the entrance corridor, directly opposite the Book of Gates. It did not make an appearance in the Valley of the Kings in the reigns that followed, though it could have been on the gilded shrines around the sarcophagi, which are now lost to us. In the tombs of Merneptah, Twosre, and Ramesses III, a variant of the concluding representation assumed a dominant position in the decoration of the sarcophagus chamber, on the upper part of the narrow right wall. The representations from the first and second sections were first employed by Ramesses IV in his third corridor, in place of the former Amduat, as was a portion of the text of the first section, which was also repeated twice in the room behind his sarcophagus chamber. An almost complete exemplar appears in the tomb of Ramesses VI, once again displayed in its entirety opposite the Book of Gates in the front half of the tomb; space limitations necessitated using the sides of some pillars in the upper pillared hall as well. The tomb of Ramesses VII displays the same arrangement on the right wall, but only in the first corridor, with a small excerpt from the first section. Finally, Ramesses IX executed selections from the first four sections on the right wall of his first and second corridors, complemented by portions of the two remaining sections in the sarcophagus chamber.

The first section, parts of the fourth section, and the concluding representation are included on the papyrus of Nedjmet from Dynasty 21. From the Late Period, the version in the tomb of Petamenophis is important and in fact indispensable, for several portions of the text are preserved only there. Fragments of a further Late Period version containing the first two sections stem from the Nilometer of Roda. The book was used only seldom on late sarcophagi, for example, CG 29306 (from Saqqara), where the first two sections are combined with the Amduat and the Litany of Re.

Research

Jean-François Champollion provided a description of the version in the tomb of Ramesses VI, along with some translations, in his thirteenth letter from Egypt. The book attracted little interest in the century that followed; eventually, the discovery of a second complete version in the

Osireion led Henri Frankfort to attempt a first translation, assisted by Adriaan de Buck, in 1933. Not until 1941–1946 did Alexandre Piankoff produce an edition of the text, drawn together from several versions, along with a translation into French; in 1954, he supplied an English translation in his edition of the tomb of Ramesses VI. The first German translation, by Erik Hornung, appeared in 1972. A synoptic edition of the text of the book has yet to be published.

Structure

An original title for the book is absent. There is no division into the regions of the night hours. An attempt is made to follow the principle of division into three registers, but space limitations often compel a staggering of the registers, and in all the versions, the first two sections have five registers. Problems also ensue from the transposition of the book to the right-hand wall in the tombs of Ramesses VI and Ramesses IX, for the original was evidently designed for a left-hand wall. Two large representations of the ram-headed sun god divide the book into two halves, each comprising three sections, making a total of six; the text of the book also alludes to these two halves. In the first and second sections, the text portions are separated from the representations, with the text placed second (the order is reversed only in the case of Ramesses VII); in each case the text presents a long monologue of the sun god in which he invokes the individual beings or groups of deities in the representation. Sections three to six again combine representations and captions, and the descriptive formula ("they are like this . . .") of the earlier books also appears. In the second half of the book, several litanies precede each of the sections; section five, with its thirteen litanies, is especially comprehensive in this regard.

As in the Book of Gates, the Book of Caverns includes, aside from the final representation, further pictures that interrupt the normal division into registers; these are the representations of Nut and Osiris in section five, with the figure of Nut alluding to the theme of the Books of the Heavens, namely, the nightly journey of the sun through the body of the sky goddess. The concluding representation contains the only indication of the solar barque, which is otherwise not found; instead, the individual scenes have a sun disk, though it is omitted from all those scenes in which the damned and their punishment are depicted, and it is also absent from the first two sections. The lower register is reserved for the damned and their punishment. The modern designation of the book derives from the fact that the netherworld is here divided into "caves" or, better, "caverns" (*qereret* in Egyptian), as in the eighth hour of the night in the Amduat. The beings who are represented in these caverns tend to be enclosed in ovals that serve, on a superficial level, as a leitmotif of the book. These are sarcophagi enclosing the corpses of gods and goddesses.

Ramesses VI enriched the text with about two hundred brief additional remarks referring to the king.

Content

The theme is once again the nightly journey of the sun god through the netherworld. Osiris is more prominent here than in the compositions discussed thus far, but the distinction between him and Re remains unclear, and both are in fact viewed as aspects of a single deity. The principal motif is Re's encounter with the corpse of Osiris in its "coffer," as laid out primarily in section three, after which the regeneration of the god commences in section four. In contrast to the Amduat and the Book of Gates, the motif of the battle with Apophis fades into the background.

At the beginning of the composition (figure 47), two vertical strips contain the solar disk and the ram-headed sun god. "Re who is in the sky" is entering into the primeval darkness with the avowed intention of caring for Osiris and sending his enemies to the slaughter. In what follows, the pictorial segment of section one is divided into five registers, while the separate text portion consists of a monologue of Re directed to the various groups of entities. Three serpents in the first cavern of the Duat guard the entrance to this realm. In the third register, Re turns directly to Osiris and extends his hand to him. Osiris is represented in a shrine that is surrounded protectively by a serpent; those in his following are also protected by serpents inside their sarcophagi. The bottom register is reserved for the enemies of Osiris, some of them already beheaded, who are guarded by another three serpents. Their punishment takes place in the depths of the Place of Annihilation, and Re condemns these enemies to nonexistence.

In section two (figure 48), Re must once again pass by several guardian serpents whose function is to restrict access, after which he reaches the gods and goddesses in their sarcophagi. In the second register he encounters forms of Osiris; in the third, the coffer of Osiris containing his corpse (figure 44) and, next to it, the ram- and jackal-headed posts of the sun god already familiar from the Book of Gates. The fourth register contains still more forms of Osiris, and in the bottom register we

44. Book of Caverns, second section with "coffer" of Osiris. From the tomb of Ramesses IV. Photo by A. Brodbeck.

once again encounter bound and decapitated enemies, some of them upside-down with their hearts torn out. Re condemns them to nonexistence, dispatching them to the Place of Annihilation, where knife-wielding guards carry out their punishment. Finally, Re tells Osiris that he intends to enter the "cavern where Aker is."

He does this in section three (figure 49), in the center of which the ithyphallic corpse of Osiris lies underneath the earth god Aker. The upper register begins with a representation of the deceased king as Osiris in his sarcophagus, guarded by two serpents. Following this are figures with the heads of catfish, who are elsewhere encountered as assistants of Aker and representatives of the dark depths of the earth and of water. Re once again encounters his own forms of manifestation, which are in sarcophagi. The end of the register is filled with divine sar-cophagi "in the cavern of Osiris-Khentamentiu." Re himself begins the middle register as the Eldest One, leaning on a staff. He encounters four forms of Osiris, the "lords of the Duat," and addresses them. Next is the central scene with the earth god Aker as a double sphinx surrounded by deities of the Ennead. Near the end of the register, the corpse of Osiris once again appears in its sarcophagus, along with the ram's head and the eye of Re in sarcophagi, all surrounded by an *ouroboros* and evi-dently stressing the unity of Re and Osiris; Osiris is depicted again, atop a serpent, as "the one who has become two." The lower register again presents enemies, all of them upside-down and some already decapi-tated. The first two groups plead for mercy, and for the first time, female enemies are depicted. All the enemies are in the primeval darkness and the Place of Annihilation, and at the end of the register, even their *ba*-souls are upside-down so as to be punished. In the midst of the enemies rests the ithyphallic corpse of Osiris; even he is in the primeval dark-ness, though he has the sun disk above him and is surrounded by a pro-tective serpent.

The second half of the Duat begins with section four (figure 50), whose beginning is somewhat altered from that of section one: between the solar disk and the ram-headed sun god is inserted an erect serpent named Great One on His Belly. The introductory text consists of three litanies in which general rejoicing once again rings out to the sun god: "How beautiful is Re, when he penetrates the darkness!" Re turns to Osiris and his following with a series of promises. At the beginning of the upper register, Isis and Nephthys lift the body of Osiris to initiate his resurrection; in the next scene, he is cared for by his two "sons," Anubis and Horus, while in the third, he appears as Bull of the West, with Horus-Mekhentienirty, the mongoose, as his son. In the middle register, the ram-headed sun god, leaning on a staff, turns to three forms of Osiris. In the two scenes that follow, Horus and Anubis appear yet again, standing in a pose symbolic of protection in front of the doubled corpse of Osiris, and in front of Osiris and his *ba*, respectively. The lower register presents the enemies as bound and standing on their heads, which this time have not been cut off; between them appear the "annihi-lators in the Place of Annihilation," with whom the "cat-formed one, from whose clutches there is no escape" is associated as a punishing demon in the first scene. It is stated of the enemies that they neither see nor hear Re, and that they have been robbed of their *ba*-souls.

Section five (figure 51) begins with further litanies that mention, inter alia, the rejuvenation of the sun by Tatenen, the god of the depths of the earth. The pictorial section opens with a large figure of Nut, the goddess of the sky, who lifts the ram-headed sun god and the solar disk on her upraised palms. She is turned toward the three registers and is framed by motifs of the course of the sun, those behind her climbing up and those in front of her going down, while arms stretched high receive the solar child. Two human-headed serpents rear up on either side of the goddess, who is designated Mysterious One and "she with the mysterious form." The upper register begins with Osiris, whose hands are stretched out to Re, and four human-headed serpents. In the second scene, Tatenen is propped up by the corpse of Atum and the corpse of Khepri. Two sarcophagi then follow, one of them containing two forms of manifestation of Re as a child. The four falcon-headed mummies at the beginning of the middle register are forms of Horus, followed by Anubis as a guardian and a coffin containing the scepter of Atum, "which created the netherworld and brought forth the realm of the dead" and thus embodies the creative power of the sun god. The register ends with four anonymous goddesses in sarcophagi. The lower register again deals with punishment, which is meted out by the female slaughterer carrying two stakes in her hands; two bound prisoners kneel next to her. Next come two scenes in which enemies are being punished in large cauldrons. The first contains their heads and hearts, and the second the decapitated, bound, upside-down enemies themselves. The "arms of the Place of Annihilation" lift the cauldrons up out of the depths while uraei fan the flames beneath them.

Behind all this, another large-scale figure interrupts the course of the registers. It is Osiris, depicted as ithyphallic, together with his *ba*, the bird atop his head; in front of him looms a protective serpent (figure 45). In the continuation of the three registers behind him, the oval containing the four "flesh" hieroglyphs again refers to the corpse of Osiris, which is cared for by the light and the voice of Re, and which is at the same time addressed as his own body and his "decay." Below, the goddess Tayt greets the sun god and Osiris; next to this, the head of Re appears in ram's form. In the lower register is another cauldron, which contains the flesh, the *ba*-souls, and the shadows of the enemies of Re and Osiris and is heated by two goddesses; we are once more in the Place of Annihilation, whose arms hold the cauldron.

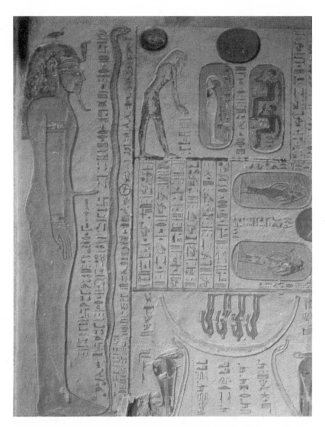

45. Book of Caverns, fifth section: figure of Osiris and cauldron in which the damned are burned. From the tomb of Ramesses IV. Photo by A. Brodbeck.

The long text between sections five and six consists of thirteen litanies that again refer to the representations in section five and in which Re addresses the entities appearing there, even his enemies. Once more, the goal of the sun god is to gaze on his corpse and effect the resurrection of Osiris-*Imenrenef*, "he whose name is hidden." The first scene in the upper register of section six (figure 52) depicts Anubis caring for corpses in their sarcophagi. The next scene is also dominated by Anubis, who tends to the sun god, represented as a ram and a falcon's head, in his sarcophagus, along with two further sarcophagi. In the third scene, two goddesses watch over forms of the sun god: the head of a ram, a scarab, and "he of the netherworld." In the last scene, Osiris-Orion bends over a mound containing a fettered and decapitated enemy, followed by a god praying before a falcon. Here, Osiris is protecting his son Horus, and in him the sun god as well. At the beginning of the middle register, a scarab beetle pushes the sun disk in front of it out from "between the two mysterious caverns of the West," which contain Osiris and Re, and they are greeted by four standing gods. The text speaks of the rebirth of the god, which is also heralded by the figure of the beetle. Even here, a last threat must be overcome, represented in the next scene as the great serpent encircling the solar beetle; the "two old and great gods in the Duat," shown in the two ovals, see to it that the serpent is placed under a spell and cut into pieces. By way of contrast, the serpent inside the mound in the third scene seems to be a regenerating one, for Re emerges from the mound in the form of a ram's head and tarries on the mound of Tatenen, which contains the tomb of this god of the depths of the earth. In the fourth scene, Re encounters two sarcophagi containing falcon-headed gods, and in the fifth scene, he meets gods with incomplete bodies; they are without their heads, which will be restored to them by the creative word of the god. The lower register again consists of scenes of punishment in the Place of Annihilation. In the first scene, goddesses armed with knives "take care of" four supine beheaded figures whose heads are set in front of their feet along with the hearts that have been torn from their bodies; according to the caption, their *ba*s and shadows are also punished. The second scene contains four bound female enemies guarded by two goddesses with jackals' heads; Re has condemned these enemies "to the Place of Annihilation, from which there is no escape." In the third scene, a god and a goddess guard four kneeling, bound enemies whose heads have been cut off. In the last scene, enemies plunge headfirst into the depths, while Osiris, surrounded by the great serpent, arises from these depths, which are again the Place of Annihilation.

A concluding representation follows (figures 46 and 52). It depicts the "two mounds" from which Re emerges, with a god bent protectively over each of them. While seven gods rejoice on either side, the solar barque is towed out of the netherworld by twelve gods; it is not yet entirely visible, but the *ba*, the scarab beetle, and the ram-headed morning form of the sun can be seen. In front of the barque, a ram-headed scarab beetle and the sun as a child also appear. Leading to a huge sun disk are two triangles composed half of black darkness and half of blue water, thus schematically summarizing the route through the netherworld. At the end of his journey, Re enters the eastern mountain, once again providing light for the world of the living.

46. Book of Caverns, concluding representation. From the tomb of Merneptah. Photo by A. Brodbeck.

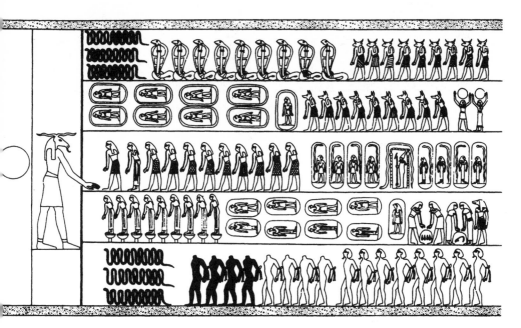

47. Book of Caverns, first section. Drawing by A. G. Shedid.

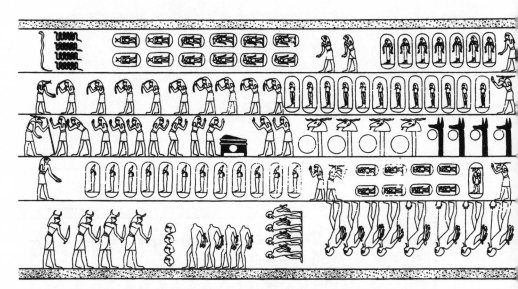

48. Book of Caverns, second section. Drawing by A. G. Shedid.

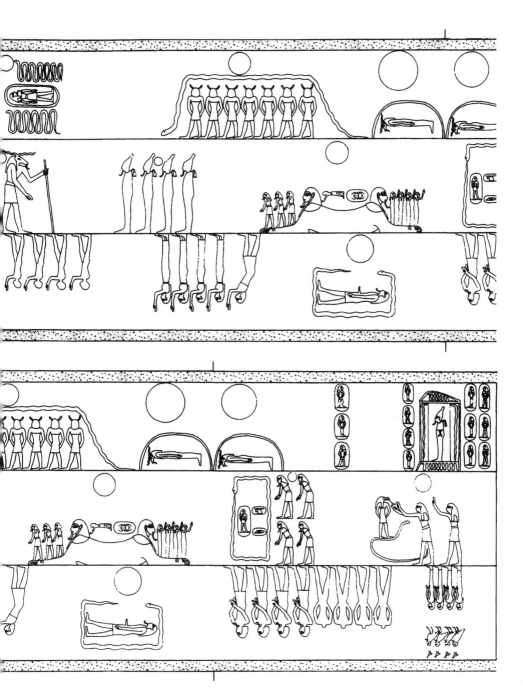

49. Book of Caverns, third section. Drawing by A. G. Shedid.

50. Book of Caverns, fourth section. Drawing by A. G. Shedid.

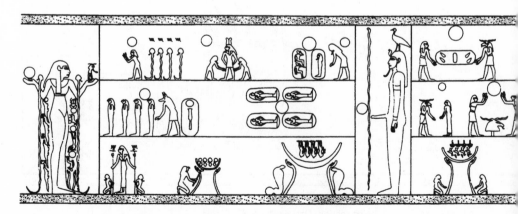

51. Book of Caverns, fifth section. Drawing by A. G. Shedid.

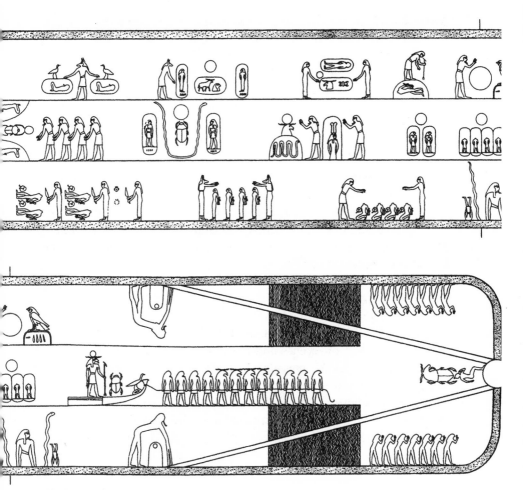

52. Book of Caverns, sixth section and concluding representation. Drawing by A. G. Shedid.

The Book of the Earth

Sources

Two scenes that would later belong to the Book of the Earth appear in the tombs of Merneptah, Twosre, and Ramesses III, on the left wall of the sarcophagus chamber, where they serve as a counterpart to the concluding representation of the Book of Caverns. Another scene, the solar barque atop Aker as a double sphinx, also occurs as an individual scene from Merneptah on, and in the tomb of Ramesses IV, it appears as the concluding representation in the decoration of the tomb. In the tomb of

Ramesses VI, all the decorated walls of the sarcophagus chamber are covered with scenes from this book, while by contrast, in the tomb of Ramesses VII only one register portrays scenes from parts D and C; finally, Ramesses IX employed two scenes from part A. The book is thus found exclusively in the sarcophagus chambers of the royal tombs; one scene is also on the sarcophagus of Ramesses IV, and it reappears on several sarcophagi of the Late Period. Individual scenes also appear in the cenotaph of Sethos I at Abydos and in the tomb of Osorkon II at Tanis. The section designated by Piankoff as the Book of Aker occurs on papyri of Dynasty 21, along with variations on the resurrection scene in A2, and in tombs of Dynasty 26 at Thebes (Petamenophis and Padineith, TT 197) and Saqqara (Lepsius 23). Additionally, from the Late Period, the representation of Nut from part D is attested in the tomb of Aba (TT 36), while the scene of the birth of the stars occurs on a cartonnage from the Ramesseum.

Research

Alexandre Piankoff laid the foundation for further study of the composition with his edition of 1953, though Jean-François Champollion had already published the scenes and texts in the sarcophagus chamber of Ramesses VI in his *Monuments de l'Égypte: Notices descriptives* (Paris, 1844, vol. 2, pp. 576–578), while part of the composition was also published by Lefébure in his *Notices des hypogées* (Cairo, 1889). In 1963 Bruno H. Stricker offered an explanation of the book in the sense of a divine embryology, while Winfried Barta and Friedrich Abitz have concerned themselves with the composition and the meaning of the book.

Structure

As in the Book of Caverns, there is no division into the hours of the night, the solar barque is largely absent as an aid to orientation, and even the division into registers is uncertain (the original probably had three registers, as usual); the overall impression is of a loose sequence of scenes. It is highly uncertain whether the tomb of Ramesses VI gives a complete exemplar; the incomplete condition of his sarcophagus chamber necessitated various transpositions of material, and as with the Book of Caverns, portions appear on the sides of several pillars. Abitz assumed that this composition, like the Book of Caverns, consists of two halves but differs, inter alia, in that only one half contains scenes of punishment. Corresponding to the Book of Caverns is the use of the sun disk as a leitmotif, with the solar barque occurring only rarely. With a few exceptions, the scenes are all oriented to the right, thus yielding a closed cycle; the sun's journey has no visible goal, nor is there an entry into the netherworld. A concluding representation is absent as well, unless we are to recognize the Aker scene on the right wall as one.

Piankoff distinguished four parts, A–D, with the division in the tomb of Ramesses VI running from right to left, contrary to the usual sequence. Abitz adds further scenes on three pillar sides as part E and makes it probable that part D, with its praying king, represents the beginning of the book, as at the beginning of the corridor of the Osireion, and that part B belongs to part A, and part C to part D. Barta, on the other hand, designates sequences of scenes from the sarcophagus chambers of Ramesses VII and Ramesses IX as part E, with the last scenes, at least, derived from a wide variety of books. In the case of Ramesses VI, part A displays a clear central axis that has perhaps led to changes in the arrangement of the scenes.

An original title is lacking for this book as well, and in this case, it has not proved easy to find a modern designation. Piankoff chose *La création du disque solaire* ("The Creation of the Sun Disk"), Hartwig Altenmüller *Buch des Aker* ("Book of Aker"), Erik Hornung *Buch von der Erde* ("Book of the Earth"), and Barta *Erdbuch* ("Earth-Book").

As was already the case in the Book of Caverns, Ramesses VI inserted many references to the king into the text and employed lines containing titles to structure it.

Content

As in the case of its external structure, the content of the book displays many affinities with the Book of Caverns, though clear differences also exist. Osiris and his coffer again play an important role, as does the transformation of Re, accompanied by the *ba*s of the blessed in his following. A special motif is the journey of the sun through the earth god Aker, which is actually an expanded version of the eleventh scene of the Book of Gates, with its "barque of the earth."

The first part (D) (figures 53 and 57) begins with a schematic representation of the entire realm of the dead, with Osiris at its center. Within a tomb structure guarded by serpents, he stands between two mounds, receiving acclamations from his *ba* and the "corpse of Geb" atop them. Below him, Anubis and the Mysterious One stretch their arms protectively over the "mysterious coffer" that invisibly contains the corpse of the god. The process of renewal taking place here is flanked by scenes of

53. Book of the Earth, part D. From the tomb of Ramesses VI. Photo by U. Schweitzer.

punishment. Cauldrons are held aloft by punishing gods whose names allude to the devouring of the bodies and the *ba*-souls of the enemies; the blood of decapitated enemies flows into the cauldrons from above, where a god holding hieroglyphs symbolizing fire concludes the scene. In the second scene, two pairs of arms rising from the depths of Nun surround a huge sun disk, on which the mummy of the sun god is standing between two fire-spitting uraei. A wreath of twelve stars and twelve small disks, whose ends are held in the hands of two goddesses, surrounds the scene and indicates the course of the hours. In the sarcophagus chamber of Ramesses III, this scene occurs in modified form: the pairs of arms are absent, and instead, the name of the king is placed in the large disk, which is surrounded by a double *ouroboros*. The third scene represents a modification of the figure of Nut in the fifth section of the Book of Caverns, with the goddess here called the Mysterious One and looking backward. The sun god is present on the palms of her hands as a ram-headed *ba*-bird and a disk. She is flanked by two human-headed serpents, and by a crocodile and yet another serpent. The last scene, which has no caption, also modifies a popular theme: the barque of the sun is depicted on the back of Aker as a double sphinx, while in the barque, which is supported by two uraei, Khepri and the ape-headed Thoth pray to the sun god. Below the barque, a winged scarab and sun disk are held on high by two anonymous royal figures, as well as by Isis and Nephthys.

The middle register begins with Horus, protected by Atum, rising up out of a recumbent divine figure called the Western One. There follow (perhaps as a separate scene) seven shrines or mounds containing gods, "those with mysterious forms," who display their faces in frontal view. The next scene repeats the motif of the miraculous, posthumous engendering of Horus. Here, falcon-headed, he emerges from the curved, supine corpse of Osiris, which is being watched over by the corpses of Isis and Nephthys. Next comes a scene with two ram-headed mummies in burial mounds; between them, two anonymous gods elevate the *ba* of Osiris, which is avian in form and adorned with the white crown. The next scene begins with the arms of Nun, which hold the solar disk. Four divine forms and two uraei flank a huge sun disk, out of which emerge a Hathor head and a serpent, both perhaps indicating the regeneration of the sun. This is also the theme of the next scene, in which a winged scarab emerges from the disk. Two praying uraei and several burial mounds containing mummies, among them that of Osiris as Bull of the West, flank the birth of the sun. The analogous scene with a sun disk and winged scarab flanked by mounds containing mummies probably also belongs in this register.

The lower register is reserved for the punishment of enemies. It begins with a figure of the sun god and several sarcophagi, followed by four enemies called the Burning Ones, who have hieroglyphs for fire instead of heads; they are watched over by four ram-headed gods. The next scene depicts four gods, each of whom seizes an enemy who is decapitated, upside-down, and painted red, perhaps meaning that he is covered with blood. Four kneeling enemies follow, with hieroglyphs for fire on their heads; they are being bound by four goddesses who "set the corpses of the enemies on fire." In a further scene, pairs of arms raise from the depths two cauldrons filled with the heads and pieces of the flesh of enemies. A fire-spitting head kindles the flames under each cauldron, while next to them, two knife-wielding gods stand by. Between them, two goddesses hold their hands protectively over a large heart. All this is occurring in the Place of Annihilation, whose "corpse" is lying in a huge sarcophagus in the next scene, and which is addressed by Re as the "corpse of Shetit," that is, of the entire realm of the dead. Above her, three gods and three goddesses raise their hands in prayer; they are in burial mounds or shrines, and their feet are hidden in the depths. In the last scene, the Apophis-serpent is being seized by ram-headed gods.

Under it, Osiris stands in a burial mound or shrine, framed by the corpse of Geb and the corpse of Tatenen; all three are sunk up to their knees in the depths.

The three registers of part C are in some way connected with part D, though the exact sequence remains undetermined. In part C (figure 56), the upper and middle registers each begin with a ram-headed sun god, to whom two *ba*-birds are praying in the upper register; the first of these is standing on a perchlike structure and the second on a scarab above the Apophis-serpent, out of whose coils Khepri is emerging, according to the caption. In front of Apophis stand Atum and Shu, whose *ba*s are perhaps intended here. In the middle register, the sun god is greeted in prayer by a god; behind him, two gods, one ram-headed and one serpent-headed, stretch out their hands protectively toward a sun disk, out of which projects the falcon's head of "Horus of the netherworld." In the lower register, four gods grasp human-headed posts; in front of them, a praying god and a praying goddess begin the register. There are four remaining scenes in part C. In the first, the corpse of Aker, depicted as a god holding a scepter, bends down over his own *ba*, which is praying to him in the form of a bird. This group is framed on either side by a burial mound containing a sun disk, out of which a praying goddess is emerging. Four Osiris figures follow, each with a sun disk behind him and a pair of arms stretched out toward him; at the end, a head is included, along with the pair of arms and sun disk. The scene containing three gods who are fettering kneeling enemies surely belongs in a lower register, as perhaps also do the three ovals that follow (one of them now destroyed), on top of which lie mummies that have turned themselves over, each with a goddess turned toward it.

The right wall, which contains part A (figures 54 and 55), begins with the sun god, "who protects the corpses," flanked by mummies in a burial mound called the Mound of Darkness. The second scene depicts the earth god Aker as a double sphinx, with the solar barque atop his mound; the barque is depicted, its direction reversed, between personifications of the entrance and the exit of the realm of the dead: the stern of the barque is facing the latter. Below is the resurrection of the corpse of the sun, a scene that occurs in the royal sarcophagus chambers beginning with Merneptah, and often later on papyri of Dynasty 21. From a falcon's head that projects out of the bottom of the sun disk, light falls on the "mysterious corpse" lying on the ground, which contains Osiris and Re in a single form; a wreath of twelve stars and twelve disks surrounds the scene, which is also framed by two Osiris figures on either side. The

54. Book of the Earth, part A. From the tomb of Ramesses VI. Photo by U. Schweitzer.

third scene depicts twelve goddesses of the hours, each with the hiero-glyphs of a star and a shadow, and each with a beaming disk above her. At the center of the fourth scene again stands a "guardian of the corpses," flanked by the figures of mummies, some of whom are in four large disks. In the fifth scene, the central god, who might be Osiris, re-mains anonymous; he is flanked by the corpses of Shu, Tefnut, Khepri, and Nun, whose *ba*-souls are traversing the darkness. In the sixth scene, a head and a pair of arms rise up from the depths. On the head stands a goddess called Annihilator, with her arms stretched out to embrace the solar disk, while on the palms of the hands of the pair of arms stand two praying goddesses named West and East, again reversed. Three mum-mies asymmetrically frame the scene.

The upper register presumably ends at this point, with a line contain-ing a title. As in the Amduat and the Book of Gates, the middle register begins with the solar barque, which is being towed by fourteen ram-headed gods, each accompanied by his *ba*. Below this scene, an ithyphal-lic god called "he who hides the hours" stands in his cave, surrounded by twelve star goddesses who extend disks to him; there are also stars and additional disks, and the figure of a child directly below the phallus of the god. Around the scene winds a great coiled serpent. The follow-ing scene is apportioned into three places in the exemplar in the tomb of

Ramesses VI; it consists of five burial mounds, out of which stretch a head and arms upraised in a gesture of praise, as well as two further mounds without a head and arms. The third scene deals with the birth of the sun and shows two erect mummies; the head of the first is a sun disk with the head and forelegs of a scarab emerging from it, while the second is topped by a praying goddess. In the fourth scene, a uraeus, a head with arms, and an upright mummy are grouped on either side of a mummiform god called "he who annihilates the hours." On the palms of the hands of each pair of arms stands another god holding a small sun disk in his hands. Expanded by yet other pictorial elements, this scene also occurs on the sarcophagus of Ramesses IV, where the theme is the birth and annihilation of the hours in the abyss of the Place of Annihilation. The top and the bottom of the fifth scene consist of ten heads each; above, they are connected to hieroglyphs denoting shadow, and below, to arms upraised in prayer. At the end, two goddesses adore the sun disk, which is moving along between these heads of the followers of the sun, accompanied by the *ba*-souls of the blessed. The lower register can be called a kind of concluding representation that summarizes the entire course of the sun. At the left, the solar barque, which contains a scarab and the ram-headed sun god, is towed by seven *ba*-birds. In the center, in changed form (raft attached to the prow, scarab adored by the *ba*s of Atum and Khepri), it passes above one head of the double sphinx Aker and into the depths, where it is received by Tatenen, god of the depths of the earth, and again released by Nun, the god of the primeval waters. In the middle, between the three (which stand for "many") mummies on either side, the arms of Nun raise the sun disk up from the depths. At the end, fourteen uraei with human heads and arms haul the barque out of the netherworld. Below the first representation of the boat, at the far left, the arms of Geb embrace a mummy called the Mourned One atop a mound containing a weeping eye and four hieroglyphs designating flesh; the indicated mourning is continued by other figures at the left. As at the end of the Amduat, the regeneration of Re is set in contrast to the mourning for Osiris.

Part B (figure 56), which has no clear division into registers, quite likely belongs to part A. First to appear are four ovals containing mummies, which breathe by means of the rays of the sun god, and four burial mounds with mummies that have turned themselves over, all under the protection of a serpent. The caption alludes to their decay, before which even Re turns away. The following scene, which stretches up the entire height of part B, is reminiscent of the representations of Nut and Osiris in the Book of Caverns; from Siptah to Ramesses IV, a sculptured version of the scene was employed on the lids of the royal sarcophagi. At the center stands the mummiform "corpse of the god," with the sun disk inside him. In front of him, a pair of arms, from which a serpent arises, holds on its palms a god and a goddess giving praise. Behind the mummy, a second pair of arms, called the "arms of the darkness," elevate the crocodile Penwenti; the hands also hold a jackal-headed and a ram-headed scepter. The ensuing four ovals containing mummies have an equal number of *ba*-birds, as well as two hieroglyphs designating shadow. Below are representations of barques containing the recumbent mummies of Osiris and the falcon-headed "Horus of the netherworld," each tended by the goddess Isis or Nephthys, respectively. At the end, the upper portion begins with a representation of a huge burial mound containing the sun disk with a god praying to it, and next to it, a large oval with two divine figures above hieroglyphic signs for flesh, framed by two heads and two goddesses, all depicted giving praise. In the lower portion are four praying gods; next to each one is a *ba*-bird and a bent hieroglyph for shadow.

Part E consists of two sides of one pillar and one side of another one in the front row of pillars; six gods in burial mounds are represented, and twice, gods pray beneath a sun disk.

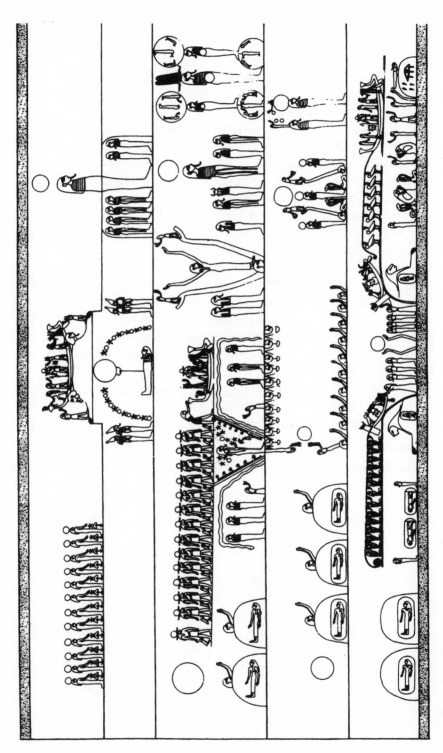

55. Book of the Earth, part A. Drawing by A. G. Shedid.

56. Book of the Earth, parts B and C. Drawing by A. G. Shedid.

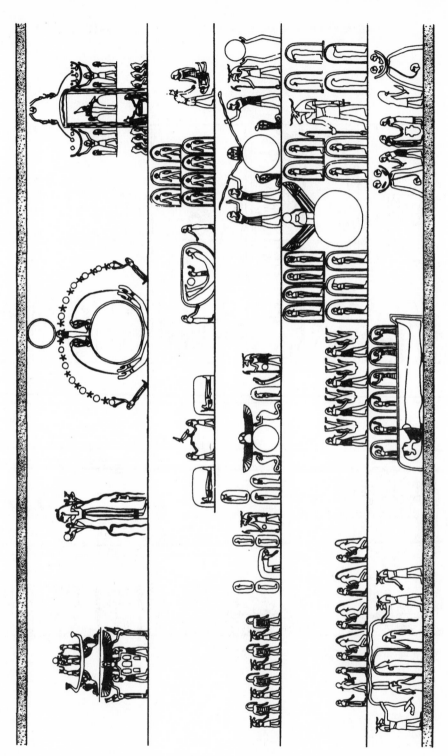

57. Book of the Earth, parc D. Drawing by A. G. Shedid.

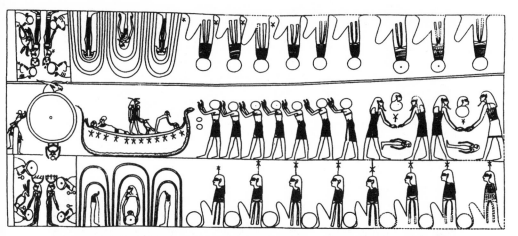

58. Ceiling of corridor G in the tomb of Ramesses VI. After A. Piankoff, *The Tomb of Ramesses VI*, ed. N. Rambova, Bollingen Series 40/1 (New York, 1954), fig. 139. Copyright © 1968, renewed 1996 by Princeton University Press.

Miscellaneous Scenes

The tombs of Ramesses VI and his successors contain a number of scenes that cannot be ascribed to any of the known Books of the Netherworld but that clearly belong to the genre of descriptions of the hereafter.

In the tomb of Ramesses VI, there are in particular representations on the ceilings, with enigmatic captions, in corridors F and G and in anteroom H preceding the sarcophagus chamber. The unusual representation of the sun barque on the ceiling of F aroused the interest of Hermann Grapow and Heinrich Schäfer, who copublished a study of it in 1937. The parallel on the ceiling of corridor C in the tomb of Ramesses IX omits this representation, but it otherwise largely corresponds to the version of Ramesses VI. In part, it seems to deal with the resurrection of the deceased, which is carried out in various stages.

The ceiling of corridor G in the tomb of Ramesses VI (figure 58) is divided into three registers, with a serpent-formed variation of the sun barque in the middle register; it is venerated by deities who have disks for heads, while the goddesses in the lower register have their disks in front of them. On the lintel of the door to anteroom H is what Friedrich Abitz has called a "protective representation" (figure 59), intended to guard against the inadvertent occurrence of a breakthrough into the neighboring tomb, KV 12.

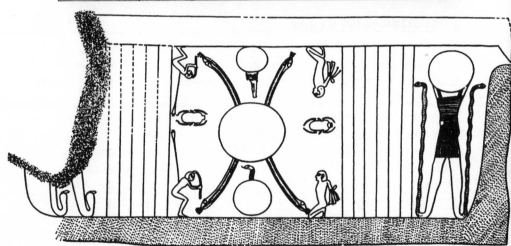

59. "Protective representation" in the tomb of Ramesses VI. Above: photo by A. Brod-beck. Below: after A. Piankoff, *The Tomb of Ramesses VI*, ed. N. Rambova, Bollingen Series 40/1 (New York, 1954), fig. 141. Copyright © 1968, renewed 1996 by Princeton University Press.

60. Scenes in the sarcophagus chamber of the tomb of Ramesses VII. Drawing by A. G. Shedid.

The ceiling of anteroom H in the tomb of Ramesses VI displays a scene of the resurrection of Osiris; parallels are found in the Osireion at Abydos and in the tomb of Petamenophis. The captions are written in part with normal hieroglyphs and in part enigmatically.

On the two side walls of the sarcophagus chamber in the tomb of Ramesses VII, two registers on each wall contain a total of seventeen scenes (figure 60). They are in part without captions, and presumably they do not belong to a single composition; the lower register on the right wall is a collection of scenes from the Book of the Earth. An overall sequence is recognizable, in so far as the left wall begins with a programmatic scene showing two figures of the sun god in his disk, while at the end of the right wall is a representation of the course of the sun. The eighth scene on the left wall depicts the nightly journey of the sun through a crocodile, for which there is a parallel on the right wall of the sarcophagus chamber of

61. "Enigmatic" wall in the tomb of Ramesses IX, right end. After F. Guilmant, *Le tombeau de Ramsès IX* (Cairo, 1907), plate 63.

Ramesses IX; here, the crocodile Penwenti might stand for the primeval waters out of which the sun emerges as a newborn child in the morning.

The left wall of the third corridor in the tomb of Ramesses IX has extracts from the Amduat. The right wall contains a series of scenes, beginning (or ending) with a scene in which the king offers a figurine depicting Maat to Ptah, along with a large diagonal figure of an ithyphallic Osiris, which is equated with Re and with the deceased king (figure 61). Next, in three registers with the solar barque in the middle register, is a composition whose organization and content connect it with the Books of the Netherworld (figure 62). The upper register remains without text, but the upside-down and spread-eagled figures depicted in its eight circles, four of which are painted red and four yellow, have been read by John C. Darnell as Lords of the Duat and explained as stars plunging downward. In the middle register, the serpent-shaped sun barque travels over the back of Apophis, while the text speaks of its coming to a standstill. Eleven serpents in front of the barque are hit by the fiery arrows of the sun's rays. The seven figures praying over the punishment

62. "Enigmatic" wall in the tomb of Ramesses IX, left end. After F. Guilmant, *Le tombeau de Ramsès IX* (Cairo, 1907), plate 63.

pits are to be understood actively, with Darnell, as "those who cast down." In the lower register appear first four goddesses subduing serpents, and then four half-upright, androgynous beings who are connected with the newborn sun as scarab and child, as well as other complex forms. The text is a variant of spell 106 of the Book of the Dead.

A sequence of scenes found on royal sarcophagi beginning with that of Siptah and on nonroyal sarcophagi of the Late Period has connections with the Book of the Earth, but it also contains scenes and texts that are independent of it. These scenes deal with the protection of the nighttime sun by the earth god, Aker, and his catfish-headed assistants; mourning; and jubilation over the sun god. They also deal with the corpse of Osiris; his union with his *ba* and the continued, posthumous effectiveness of the sexual potency of the god of the dead; and with the birth and the annihilation of the hours, which fall into the abyss of the Place of Annihilation. Ramesses IV employed the sequence dealing with the sun god twice on his sarcophagus, thereby omitting the sequence dealing with Osiris.

THE BOOKS OF THE SKY

After the Amarna Period, a new group of Books of the Afterlife took shape. These center on a representation of the sky goddess, Nut, transposing the nightly journey of the sun into her body and thus into a celestial hereafter. The goddess Nut gives birth to the sun god in the morning. During the day, he passes visibly along her body and is "swallowed" by her mouth in the evening. From there, during the night, he journeys invisibly back to the place where he will rise again. Yet the sun god travels through the same landscape already familiar from the Books of the Netherworld, and the same or similar motifs appear in both realms; this celestial hereafter corresponds in every way to the netherworldly one.

From Ramesses IV on, two Books of the Sky tended to be placed next to each other on the ceilings of the royal tombs; these are distinctive because of the double representation of the sky goddess, depicted back-to-back (figure 63). Although the focus is on the course of the sun, the other heavenly bodies are also included, in particular the decans. On the whole, the books emphasize cosmography and the topography of the sky, which already had their beginnings in the Book of the Heavenly Cow (see the next chapter, "Special Compositions"). The combination of the Book of Nut and the Book of the Night, as they appear on the ceilings of the cenotaph of Sethos I at Abydos and the tomb of Ramesses IV, was employed again in Dynasty 26 in the tomb of Mutirdis (TT 410). The

63. Book of the Day and Book of the Night. From the tomb of Ramesses VI. Photo by U. Schweitzer.

"astronomical ceilings," as first found in the tomb of Senenmut and then in those of Sethos I to Ramesses III, on the ceilings above the sarcophagus of the king, can be viewed as their precursors. In a further development after the New Kingdom, representations and texts were added to the changing forms of the sun god in the individual hours of the day and the night.

The Book of Nut

Sources

From the New Kingdom, the Book of Nut is attested only in the cenotaph of Sethos I at Abydos and in the tomb of Ramesses IV; in the latter, the version is abridged. In each case, the book is on the ceiling of the sarcophagus chamber. From the Roman Period (mid-second century C.E.), a commentary on the book is written in Demotic (P. Carlsberg 1 and 1a). In the interval, only the tomb of Mutirdis (TT 410) from Dynasty 26 (c. 630–620 B.C.E.) offers even an incomplete version, one that is apparently related to that of Ramesses IV. No further versions are known to date.

Research

Jean-François Champollion and Hippolito Rosellini published early drawings of the representation of the sky goddess, and Heinrich Brugsch also offered a transcription in his *Thesaurus;* these were all copies of Ramesses IV's version, for that in the Osireion was not discovered until 1914. The Demotic commentary was published in 1940 by H. O. Lange and Otto Neugebauer. In 1960, Neugebauer and Richard A. Parker included all the sources in volume 1 of their *Egyptian Astronomical Texts.* More recently, discussion has centered on the astronomical aspects of the representation and its table of decans.

Structure and Language

The book functions as a pictorial description, and in this, it resembles the Book of the Heavenly Cow. Visually, the brief captions seem to recede beside the huge, dominating representation of the sky (figure 64). The sky goddess Nut is depicted in the form of a woman supporting herself on the ground, which does not yet appear as the earth god, Geb, on her hands (which are correctly on the right, thus in the west, in the cenotaph of Sethos I, though they are on the left in the tomb of Ramesses IV) and her feet, while the god Shu holds her body aloft. There are complementary pictorial motifs, such as several sun disks, a winged scarab in front of the knees of the goddess, a vulture atop the heraldic plant of Upper Egypt behind her legs, and nests of migratory birds next to her arms. A longer appended text complements the brief captions to the representation. Papyrus Carlsberg reproduces the original text (a representation either is lacking or was at the beginning and has been lost) in hieratic script, along with a translation into Demotic and a commentary that is also written in Demotic.

Content

The illustration and its captions are intended to supply both a topography of the sky and an understanding of the daily course of the sun. The brief captions are distributed over the entire representation, describing its details as well as the actions of the sun god, the decans, and other divine beings. Text L supplies an important definition of the "far regions of this sky": they are in the primeval darkness and the primeval waters, inaccessible to the sun, with unknown boundaries and the cardinal directions nullified. Texts S through X give a list of decans, which perhaps goes back to a Middle Kingdom original, and speak of their "work" and their periodic invisibility, while texts Dd to Ff treat the migratory birds and their nests. With regard to the decan stars, consideration is given not to their rising but rather to their transit through the meridian.

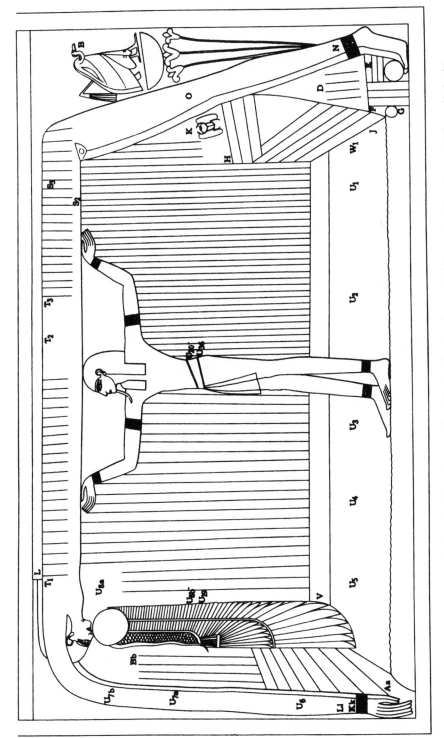

64. Book of Nut (Cenotaph of Sethos I). After O. Neugebauer and R. A. Parker, *Egyptian Astronomical Texts*, vol. I (Providence, 1960), p. 40, fig. 21.

In the version from the cenotaph of Sethos I and in the late version, the end of the text is a "dramatic text" reporting a quarrel between Geb and Nut because she kept "swallowing" their children, the stars. Their common father, Shu, settled the dispute by advising that the stars be born again each time so that they might live. On each occasion, however, they were to remain for seventy days in the House of Geb, and thus invisible in the netherworld, in order to be regenerated there.

The Book of the Day

Sources

The only New Kingdom tomb in which the Book of the Day (figures 65–71) has been found to date is that of Ramesses VI. It reappears in the royal necropolis at Tanis; there are selections in the tomb of Osorkon II, and a nearly complete version exists in that of Shoshenq III. The latest versions occur in the tomb of the scribe Ramose (TT 132) from the reign of Taharqa of Dynasty 25, to which should be added the brief texts regarding the hours of the day on certain sarcophagi and papyri of the Late Period, which are perhaps from a related source, as well as the hymns to the hours of the day in the pronaos of the temple of Edfu.

Research

The versions in the sarcophagus chamber and the preceding corridors in the tomb of Ramesses VI were copied by Jean-François Champollion, but for a long time they attracted no interest. Only in 1942 did Alexandre Piankoff publish his edition, though it lacked the versions in the tombs at Tanis discovered in 1939–1940. In the meantime, further attention has been paid only to the hymn to the second hour, which was employed in temples, and a thorough, fresh study is lacking.

Structure and Language

The representations and captions of the book are arranged under an extended figure of the sky goddess Nut, whose arms and legs comprise their outer limit. Nearly all the figures face the head of Nut and thus the end of the book. In principle, the text follows the course of the twelve hours; it is not split up vertically, however, but rather arranged horizontally into five registers, with the result that it remains unclear where one hour ends and the next begins. This arrangement is not followed at the beginning and the end, where a prologue and a concluding representation, respectively, stand out from the main portion. An original title is absent. It is possible that the Book of the Day and the Book of the Night belong together, forming a unity, but they occur together only in the tomb of Ramesses VI (see figure 61), on the ceiling of his sarcophagus chamber and in the preceding portion (C to E) of the tomb.

Content

Unlike the other books, the Book of the Day describes the diurnal, not the nocturnal, journey of the sun, which travels from the vulva of the goddess, from which it is newly born each day (figure 65), to her head, which swallows it again in the evening. Because the reference here is to the daytime journey of the sun god, he appears with a falcon's head rather than in his ram-headed nocturnal form; nevertheless, netherworldly motifs such as the repulsing of Apophis and the Field of Reeds occur as focal points in the middle of the composition. The texts and representations consist mainly of an enumeration of deities, with few descriptive texts; additionally, the hymns to the hours can be explained as the liturgical portion of the book.

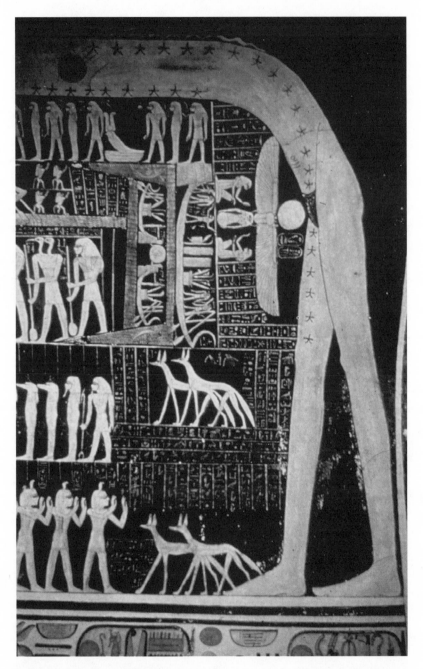

65. Book of the Day, rebirth of the sun. From the tomb of Ramesses VI. Photo by U. Schweitzer.

66. Book of the Day, beginning. After A. Piankoff, *The Tomb of Ramesses VI*, ed. N. Rambova, Bollingen Series 40/1 (New York, 1954), fig. 130. Copyright © 1968, renewed 1996 by Princeton University Press.

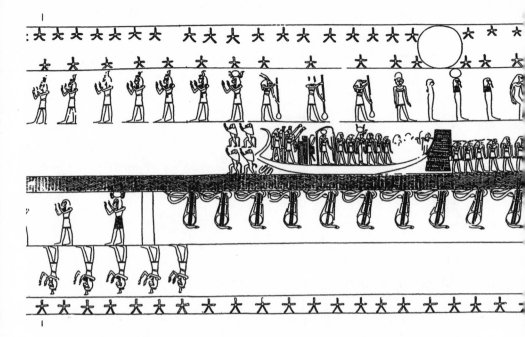

67. Book of the Day, extract. After A. Piankoff, *The Tomb of Ramesses VI*, ed. N. Rambova, Bollingen Series 40/1 (New York, 1954), fig. 130. Copyright © 1968, renewed 1996 by Princeton University Press.

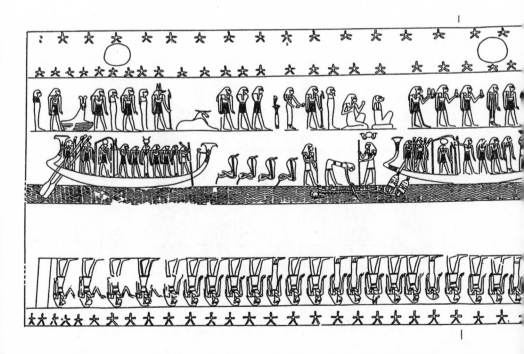

68. Book of the Day, extract depicting Apopis. After A. Piankoff, *The Tomb of Ramesses VI*, ed. N. Rambova, Bollingen Series 40/1 (New York, 1954), fig. 131. Copyright © 1968, renewed 1996 by Princeton University Press.

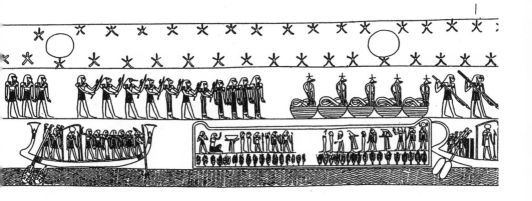

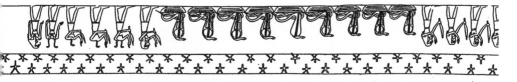

69. Book of the Day, extract depicting the Field of Reeds. After A. Piankoff, *The Tomb of Ramesses VI*, ed. N. Rambova, Bollingen Series 40/1 (New York, 1954), fig. 133. Copyright © 1968, renewed 1996 by Princeton University Press.

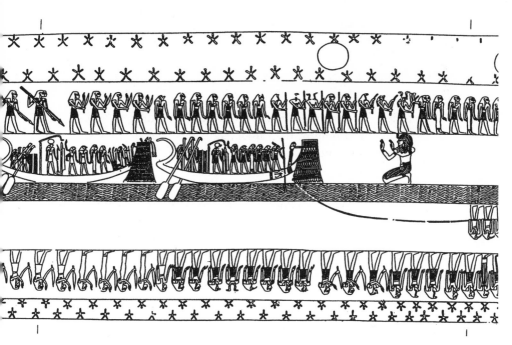

70. Book of the Day, last hour. After A. Piankoff, *The Tomb of Ramesses VI*, ed. N. Rambova, Bollingen Series 40/1 (New York, 1954), fig. 133. Copyright © 1968, renewed 1996 by Princeton University Press.

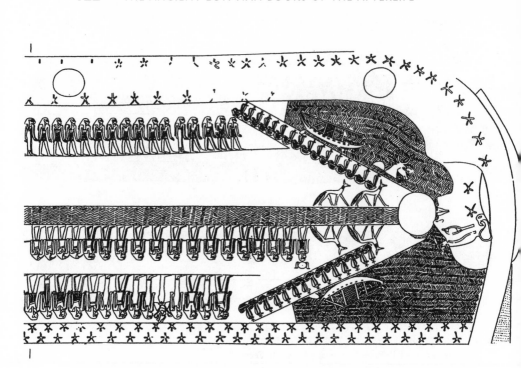

71. Book of the Day, conclusion. After A. Piankoff, *The Tomb of Ramesses VI*, ed. N. Rambova, Bollingen Series 40/1 (New York, 1954), fig. 132. Copyright © 1968, renewed 1996 by Princeton University Press.

The Book of the Night

Sources

The earliest version of the Book of the Night (figures 72–84), that of Sethos I on the ceiling of the sarcophagus chamber of the Osireion at Abydos, reaches only the ninth hour; Merneptah had a second version placed on the ceiling of the antechamber, but only a few traces remain. Later, Ramesses IV placed this book next to the Book of Nut on the ceiling of his sarcophagus chamber, though for reasons of space, it breaks off with the fourth hour. Only the tomb of Ramesses VI provides two complete versions; one is on the west side of the ceiling of the sarcophagus chamber, while the other is spread out over the ceilings of C, D, and E (the book up to the eighth hour is in E, the ninth and tenth hours are in D, and the eleventh and twelfth hours are in C), and in both cases they complement the Book of the Day. Additionally, representations from the book are employed on the ceiling of F and in the tomb of Ramesses IX, on the ceilings of the second and third corridors and the sarcophagus chamber. On the whole, the book appears only on ceilings in the New Kingdom (carved in relief in Sethos I's version and otherwise painted), and its location did not shift to the walls until the royal tombs at Tanis. Osorkon II again combined it with the Book of the Day, while Shoshenq III followed Sethos I's version closely.

In the Late Period (Dynasties 25–26), extracts appear in some tombs at Thebes (TT 33, 132, and 410) and on fragments from the Nilometer at Roda. Later still, they appear on sarcophagi from Dynasty 30 and the early Ptolemaic Period (Cairo CG 29305, J. 48446/47, and J. 48861; Berlin 49; Louvre D 8 and D 9; Vienna 5), where they are combined with hours from the Amduat.

The text from the second hour of the night also appears in the solar sanctuaries of Deir el-Bahri and Medinet Habu and in the edifice of Taharqa at Karnak.

Research

Jean-François Champollion laid the initial foundation with his copies of both versions in the tomb of Ramesses VI, and Eugène Lefébure added Ramesses IV's version in 1889. The version in the cenotaph of Sethos I at Abydos was discovered by Edouard Naville only in 1914, and it was published by Henri Frankfort in 1933. Alexandre Piankoff's edition, which appeared in 1942, took these foundations into account as well as some versions from the Late Period, but not the tombs at Tanis, which had been discovered only in 1939–1940. His edition has now been completely replaced by that of Gilles Roulin. There is as yet no translation into German.

Structure and Language

The book is divided into twelve sections separated from one another by vertical lines of text designated as "gates"; in contrast to the Book of Gates, these precede the hours of the night to which they belong. The arms and the legs of the goddess represent the first and last gates; the first hour is not represented. Each hour has an introductory text containing the most important details, while the remaining texts are mostly just brief captions. The vertical arrangement contains three registers (staggered into five to seven registers for reasons of space, though only two appear in the tomb of Osorkon II), with the sun barque journeying through the middle one. In the barque, the sun god is surrounded by the many-coiled *Mehen*-serpent while another serpent protects him within his shrine. The crew consists of Sia at the prow as spokesman of the god, as in the Book of Gates; Hu at the stern; and Maat; in the version of Sethos I at Abydos, the king also appears. The upper register depicts deities of the hereafter both individually and collectively, while the lower one displays various groups of deceased persons, both the blessed and the damned. In each case, the solar barque is preceded by a rather large group—as many as thirty and more—of towmen called the Un-wearying Ones; they are led by the king, who is here included in the representation. Descriptive texts like those characteristic of the Books of the Netherworld are lacking here, and as a rule, the registers are not divided into scenes. As in the Books of the Netherworld, at the end is a summary of the entire course of the sun.

Content

Complementing the Book of the Day, the sun god's journey here extends from the point where he is swallowed by the sky goddess in the evening to his rebirth in the morning in the form of a scarab. During his journey, the god has his ram-headed nocturnal form and, as in the Amduat, he is designated as flesh. The arrangement by means of gates already represents an analogy with the Books of the Netherworld, and motifs otherwise familiar from these compositions also occur. Even Tatenen, the god of the depths of the earth, appears here in the celestial hereafter. As in the Book of Gates, Sia plays an active role and appears as the spokesman of the sun god. The latter also has his own escort in the middle register of each hour (crocodile-headed in the last three) in place of the hour goddesses who accompany him in the Amduat and the Book of Gates.

The remnants of an introduction are preserved only in Sethos I's version, wherein the sun god furnishes a programmatic explanation of the goal of his journey through the hereafter, which has to do with judging the damned and caring for the blessed dead. As at the beginning of the Amduat, the primeval darkness is mentioned as a border area. The first hour of the night is not represented; as in the Amduat and the Book of Gates, it was viewed as an interstitial area, to be thought of here as situated between the arms of Nut. The actual beginning is the second hour, where the upper register endeavors to include not only individual deities but groups of them as well: the deities of the four cardinal points, the *bas* of Buto and Hierakonpolis, and the two Enneads, which stand for the totality of all divine beings. In the upper register of the seventh hour general figures also appear, representing existence and nonexistence. Opposite them are the totality of the deceased in the lower register, who appear as the "transfigured ones" (*akhu*), mummies, and the "dead," that is, the damned.

The motif of the union of Re and Osiris is absent, though the representation of *ba*s and corpses in the lower register of the sixth hour serves to indicate the longed-for union in the depths of the night, with which the regeneration in the seventh hour is connected. This critical moment once again requires the overcoming of enemies, here imaged concretely as their incineration. The lower register of the seventh hour (figure 77) also takes up a theme that made its appearance in the thirtieth scene of the Book of Gates: Horus turns to both foreigners (depicted as Asiatics, Libyans, Medja bedouins, and Nubians) and Egyptians (depicted as dwellers in the fertile land and in the desert), though here the foreigners do not have the same status as Egyptians but are again seen as bound enemies. The speech of the god also includes motifs from the twenty-first scene of the Book of Gates.

The lower register of the eighth hour (figure 78) is dominated by an enthroned Osiris, with Horus and the other gods of his circle in attendance. Osiris is triumphing over a well-fettered enemy, here anonymous but whom the versions of the Late Period address directly as Seth. The various groups of deceased, both the blessed and the damned, are turned in prayer toward this scene, and their representation continues in the ninth hour (figure 79); there, they are addressed by Sia, who announces their fates in the afterlife, stressing at the same time their attachment to Osiris. Only blessed dead appear in the lower register of the tenth hour (figure 80).

In the twelfth and last hour (figures 82–83), the towmen in front of the barque are augmented by four jackals designated "Western *ba*s," as at Medinet Habu. The deities in the lower register, among them Osiris, are turned in prayer toward the concluding representation (figure 84), which summarizes the entire course of the sun, as in the Books of the Netherworld. Here, with the help of the primeval gods, the nocturnal sun god is transformed into a scarab and a child; behind these are the two barques of his daytime and nighttime journeys, along with Isis and Nephthys, who were later placed in the prow of the barque, keeping the sun in constant motion between them. The accompanying cosmographical text also refers to the totality of the course of the sun god, identifying his three cosmic realms as the netherworld (Duat), the primeval waters (Nun), and the sky (Nut).

Striking is the considerable prominence of the king—especially in the version of Sethos I—who appears at the head of those towing the sun

(*text continues p. 135*)

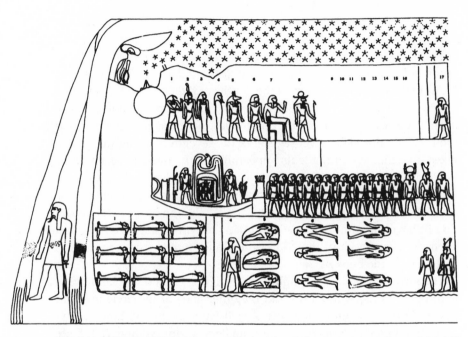

72. Book of the Night, first and second hours. After G. Roulin, *Le Livre de la nuit*, OBO 147 (Freiburg and Göttingen, 1996), pt. II, plate I.

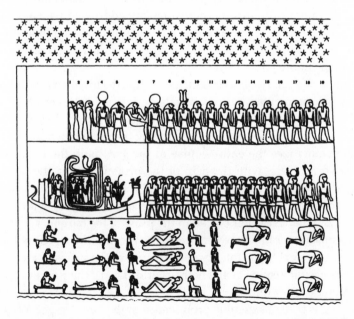

73. Book of the Night, third hour. After G. Roulin, *Le Livre de la nuit*, OBO 147 (Freiburg and Göttingen, 1996), pt. II, plate III.

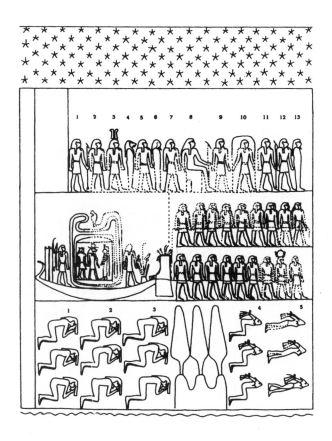

74. Book of the Night, fourth hour. After G. Roulin, *Le Livre de la nuit*, OBO 147 (Freiburg and Göttingen, 1996), pt. II, plate V.

75. Book of the Night, fifth hour. After G. Roulin, *Le Livre de la nuit*, OBO 147 (Freiburg and Göttingen, 1996), pt. II, plate VI.

76. Book of the Night, sixth hour. After G. Roulin, *Le Livre de la nuit*, OBO 147 (Freiburg and Göttingen, 1996), pt. II, plate VIII.

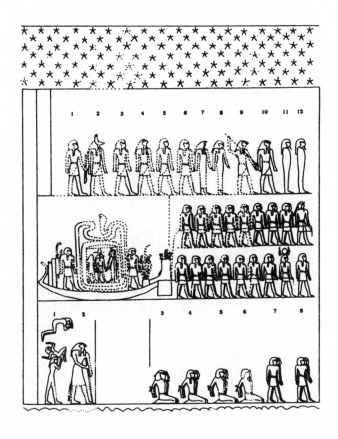

77. Book of the Night, seventh hour. After G. Roulin, *Le Livre de la nuit*, OBO 147 (Freiburg and Göttingen, 1996), pt. II, plate IX.

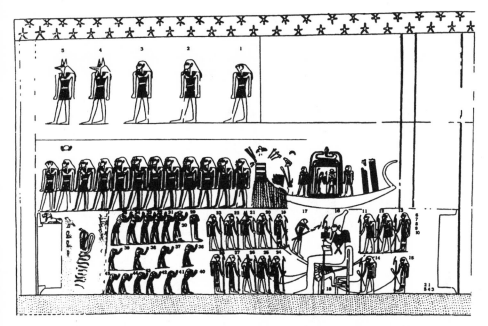

78. Book of the Night, eighth hour. After G. Roulin, *Le Livre de la nuit*, OBO 147 (Freiburg and Göttingen, 1996), pt. II, plate XII.

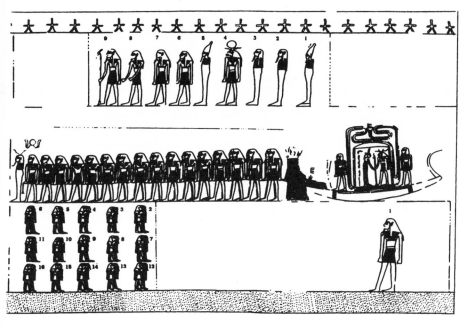

79. Book of the Night, ninth hour. After G. Roulin, *Le Livre de la nuit*, OBO 147 (Freiburgand Göttingen, 1996), pt. II, plate XIV.

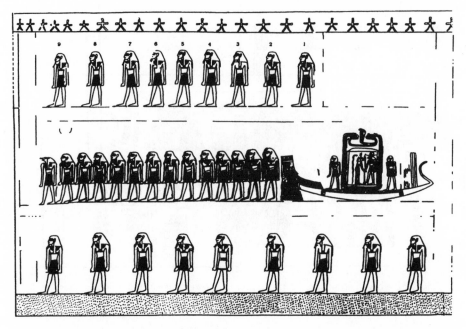

80. Book of the Night, tenth hour. After G. Roulin, *Le Livre de la nuit*, OBO 147 (Freiburg and Göttingen, 1996), pt. II, plate XVI.

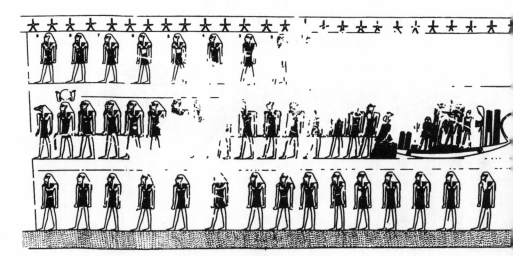

81. Book of the Night, eleventh hour. After G. Roulin, *Le livre de la nuit*, OBO 147 (Freiburg and Göttingen, 1996), pt. II, plate XVII.

82. Book of the Night, twelfth hour. After G. Roulin, *Le Livre de la nuit*, OBO 147 (Freiburg and Göttingen, 1996), pt. II, plate XVIII.

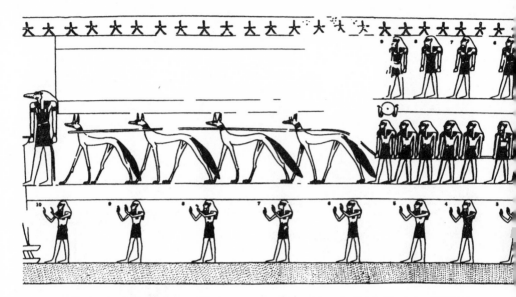

83. Book of the Night, twelfth hour, continuation. After G. Roulin, *Le Livre de la nuit*, OBO 147 (Freiburg and Göttingen, 1996), pt. II, plate XIX.

84. Book of the Night, concluding representation. After G. Roulin, *Le Livre de la nuit*, OBO 147 (Freiburg and Göttingen, 1996), pt. II, plate XX.

barque in every hour of the night. In contrast to the Book of the Day, the sun's enemy Apophis appears nowhere in this book; the repelling of the inimical Seth is mentioned several times instead. At the end is a description of the "Western *ba*s," who tow the sun god into the sky, where his birth from Nut is also viewed as his emergence from the netherworld (Duat).

SPECIAL COMPOSITIONS

The Litany of Re

Sources

Portions of the Litany of Re occur in the tombs of Tuthmosis III and his vizier, Useramun, with the excerpts evidently related to one another. The series of figures to the "Great Litany" also appear in both tombs, but there are no further illustrations. The entire text, with a few omissions, first occurs on the shroud dedicated by Amenophis II to his father, Tuthmosis III. The subsequent disappearance of the book is especially striking in the case of Tutankhamun, for all the burial equipment in his tomb has been preserved to us. The book is attested again under Sethos I, in whose tomb the figure to the title first appears. From then on, the book was the standard decoration in the first and second corridors of the royal tombs; Ramesses VI was the first to give it up in its entirety, though Ramesses IX and Ramesses X again included extracts. The figures were always reserved for the second corridor, while the text filled the first corridor with a little of it reaching into the second corridor. In the tombs of Sethos I and Ramesses II, all the hieroglyphs face the interior of the tomb, whereas from Merneptah on, they face uniformly to the right so that all the columns of text are reversed. A portion of the figures appears in Merneptah's decoration in the Osireion of Sethos I at Abydos, and the complete sequence occurs in the temple built at that site by

Ramesses II. In the Late Period, the figures were used in temples (the edifice of Taharqa and the chapel of Hakoris at Karnak) and also in tombs (Mentuemhet, Petamenophis, Ibi, and the fragments from the Nilometer at Roda) and on papyri and sarcophagi. The textual tradition breaks off with the sarcophagi from the early Ptolemaic Period.

Already in Dynasty 18, excerpts were adopted as spell 127 of the Book of the Dead, beginning with the manuscript of Maiherperi, and as spell 180 in early Dynasty 19, starting with the sarcophagus of Sethos I. The well-known representation of the ram-headed Re-Osiris in the tomb of Nefertari and in other tombs of Dynasty 19 actually belongs to this spell of the Book of the Dead and not to the Litany of Re.

Research

Richard Pococke published an early description of the version in the tomb of Ramesses IV in his account of his travels. Text editions of the Litany of Re were among the earliest in the field of Egyptology. In 1869, Edouard Naville took up the texts of the Litany in the tombs of Sethos I and Ramesses IV and published them with a translation into French in 1875; an English translation by him appeared in 1876. For a century, his edition remained the basis for scholarly concern with the book. Alexandre Piankoff's edition of 1964 contains no hieroglyphic texts (his hand copies seem to have been lost), but there are photographs from several tombs, especially those of Sethos I and Sethos II, and of the shroud of Tuthmosis III, along with a translation into English. Before that, Hermann Grapow concerned himself with the text and figures in a paper in *ZÄS* 72 (1936). Erik Hornung then included all the New Kingdom versions in a commentary volume in his edition of 1975.

Structure

In contrast to the Books of the Netherworld, this book bears an original title, which already appears in the tomb of Useramun as "Book of Praying to Re in the West, Praying to the United One in the West"; remarks concerning the recitation and efficacy of the text are also included. The text begins with the Great Litany, wherein the sun god is invoked seventy-five times in various names and forms; the first verse of each invocation is "Praise to you, oh Re, great of power." Aside from this litany, only the sixth ("Oh, Re, come to me, leader . . .") is composed in verses, while the text on the ceiling of the second corridor stands out, because of its location, as a further, independent section; it already appears separately in the tomb of Tuthmosis III. The structure of the remainder of the text is not as clear; only the litanies (which number nine in all) are distinct because of their unique initial refrains.

The divine figures that illustrate each of the invocations in the Great Litany belong to the early content of the book. From the very beginning, these figures were split up so that they alternate in two series—for example, they face one another on the north and south walls of the tomb of Useramun, while in the Ramesside tombs, they are on both walls of the second corridor, with the left wall taking precedence (it is the other way around in the case of Useramun). The figures follow a strict alternation up to the fifty-first invocation, with the odd-numbered figures on the left and the even-numbered figures on the right. The arrangement is then interrupted by two successive figures (51 and 52) on the left and two (53 and 54) on the right. A regular alternation then resumes, though in reverse sequence, with the even-numbered figures on the left and the odd-numbered figures on the right. Thus, as so often occurs, a strict regularity is avoided.

Determining the exact number of figures is complicated. The text speaks of seventy-four "forms" (*kheperu*), and that many are also depicted (with numbers 23 and 67 as plurals, and thus tripled), with the ram-headed *ba* of Re in its sun disk (the sixth figure on the left) not attached to an invocation and the only figure facing in the opposite direction. But because each of the last two figures of the left-hand series has two names ascribed to it, we can actually assume seventy-six figures, which, with the additional *ba* of Re, belong to the seventy-five invocations. Either way, the oft-noted parallel to the seventy-five serpents of the Story of the Shipwrecked Sailor seems plausible, and the tomb of Sethos I also seems to intimate a relationship with the seventy-five scenes of the Opening of the Mouth ritual. The symbolism of this number, however, remains uncertain.

The seventy-five invocations can be understood as three times twenty-five, with special emphasis on the twenty-sixth and the fifty-first. There are also groups of ten, with the first ten differing in structure from the rest, while the following group of ten is reserved for an extended Ennead.

The two sequences are constantly divided between the gods Re and Osiris, just as the union of these two gods receives special treatment in the text. In fact, figures of Osiris are found only in the sequence on the left, while on the right, the many scarab-beetles are striking. But also appearing on the left are Atum, the *ba* of Re, and the Great Cat, though traditionally the left side belongs to the sun god and the right to Osiris, especially in the rows on the ceiling of the first corridor in the royal tombs but also in the opposition of Re and Sokar in the tomb of Ramesses VII. Since a union is of concern here, a transient merging of the two gods with each other, a strict division would in any case make little sense and would spring rather from an anachronistically modern attempt at a schematic division. Instead, elements relating to Re and Osiris are inextricably intermingled in both sequences, though Re and Osiris themselves do not appear as figures.

The names and the figures that illustrate them refer to the most important forms and functions of the sun god in the netherworld. Thus, there occur his morning form of Khepri (three times); his evening form of Atum; the *ba* of Re (as an additional figure, also at the beginning of the text on the ceiling, starting with Merneptah); his forms of ram, cat, and child; the divine Eye; and the sun disk, as well as the accompanying figure of a baboon. In addition to Atum, the remaining gods and goddesses of the Ennead make their appearance, though Seth is replaced by Horus. Of the primeval gods, Nun and Tatenen—the watery depths and the depths of the earth—are represented. Osiris appears only as Khentamentiu, though two names refer to the union of the two gods, which represents a central theme of the entire litany.

Several names, incidentally, stress the god's close connection with the netherworldly realm of the dead; thus, he is called "he of the netherworld," "he of the cave," "he who has command over his cave," "he who renews the earth," and even directly, "the West." Further names designate him as one who travels through this sphere, and in the concluding text of the Great Litany, he is even called "migratory bird." Rejoicing and mourning are both represented, for death and rebirth are the concern here, and certain names make reference to the corpse of the god, and even to its decay, which must precede his regeneration. The double aspect of the nighttime sun is represented by the juxtaposition of light and sunbeams on the one hand and covering and darkness on the other. Finally, the god's beneficent deeds for the blessed dead are mentioned, but so is his function as punisher of the damned.

Already in the tomb of Useramun, the divine figures are supplemented by additional depictions. The vizier placed his own figure at the end of both sequences, and his wife and other members of his family are also at the end of the left-hand sequence. Tuthmosis III, who distributed the two sequences over the two pillars of his sarcophagus chamber, had himself and female members of his family represented on an adjoining side of one of the pillars. In his temple at Abydos, Ramesses II expanded the sequence of figures to include royal ancestors—his parents and his grandfather, as well as the founder of the New Kingdom—but he himself, like Merneptah in the Osireion, is represented only making offerings to them, while the figures taken together thereby become the object of cult worship (even the inimical eighth figure), which also explains their presence in the temple. Beginning with this version, the figures also contain a small sun disk to indicate the presence of the sun god within them.

Already under Ramesses IX, and then in Dynasty 21, sarcophagi were decorated with a combination of divine figures from the litany and altogether different deities, thus creating a dense wall of protection around the deceased; in an analogous manner, this also occurred on funerary papyri. Thus over time, the figures, which began as mere illustrations to the invocations, themselves became "gods who are in the West" (as they are called in the monuments of Mentuemhet and Hakoris), and in the chapel of Hakoris, their names all have divine determinatives.

Beginning with the version of Sethos I, a further representation, a "title illustration" (figures 85 and 87), is inserted between the title of the book and the Great Litany. It is programmatic in character, depicting a scarab and a ram-headed god in a disk, before whom inimical theriomorphic powers—a serpent and an antelope above, and a crocodile and an antelope below—are in flight on either side. In a recent interpretation, John C. Darnell has proposed that the animals have been dispatched by the sun god against his enemies and that they are therefore accompanying him as bodyguards.

On an ad hoc basis, a representation of the united Re and Osiris was added in the tomb of Nefertari (figure 86); as an illustration however, it does not belong to the Litany of Re itself but rather to spell 180 of the Book of the Dead; thus it also occurs in the tombs of some royal officials of Dynasty 19 and, in QV 40, the tomb of an anonymous queen.

Two spells of the Book of the Dead, 127 and 180, adopted portions of the Litany of Re. In contrast, nothing from the actual Books of the Netherworld is to be found in the Book of the Dead, except for the special case of spell 168. In spell 127, the "gods in the caverns" are invoked and associated with the guardians of the gates of the netherworld; there

85. Litany of Re, title illustration. From the tomb of Siptah. Photo by A. Wiese.

86. Re and Osiris united. From the tomb of Queen Nefertari. Photo by A. Brack.

is a corresponding combination of the two groups in the temple of Ramesses II at Abydos. In spell 127, we also find the sole mention of the Place of Annihilation in the Book of the Dead. The spell is already attested in the Book of the Dead of Maiherperi, and thus in the reign of Amenophis II, and later, on P. Busca and in the tombs of Ramesses IV and Ramesses VI. Spell 180 begins with the central verse, "It is Re, who rests in Osiris," and a part of its title is "Praying to Re in the West." This spell is attested on the coffin of Sethos I, and in part in the Osireion, and also in the tomb of an official (TT 3) and on papyri (Qenna, Neferrenpet, Louvre 3073) from the end of Dynasty 18 and the beginning of Dynasty 19.

The earlier distinction between a "greater" and a "lesser" litany (e.g., Hermann Grapow, ZÄS 72, 1936: 15) is no longer regarded as accurate.

Content

The book begins the decoration of the royal tombs of the Ramesside Period, and its importance is also indicated by the fact that after his victory over the usurper Amenmesse, Sethos II ordered the Litany of Re hacked out of the tomb begun by Amenmesse so as to do harm to him in his posthumous existence. This composition is a description and a praise of that deity who descends into the netherworld at night, awakens the dead to renewed life, cares for the blessed, and punishes the damned. The multitude of figures and functions of the nocturnal sun god in the Great Litany opens up the entire netherworld to the deceased. At the same time there exists a desire to include the deceased king in the course of the sun, thus assuring his daily regeneration. This connection with the course of the sun also explains why the text accompanying the united Re-Osiris is included in the illustration of Book of the Dead spell 109, in which the sun is called a newborn calf, in the tomb of Arinefer (TT 290).

Re is viewed as a migratory bird that visits the netherworld each night and there becomes, like all the dead, a cavern dweller, as he is called in the concluding text of the Great Litany. Immediately after that, the deceased speaks for the first time, stressing that he has a thorough knowledge of Re's nocturnal forms of manifestation and their names; he adds his hope that they will open the netherworld for him and his *ba*, since he is indeed the image of the sun god and his *ba*. That the deceased himself speaks here, or is referred to in the third person, distinguishes this text from the Books of the Netherworld.

This concluding text is followed by the second litany, in which the in-habitants of the netherworld are commanded to prepare the way for the deceased in the following of Re. Interrupted only by an invocation to the nocturnal sun, "who shines among those in the netherworld," the third litany adds, "May you lead me to the ways of the West." This formula-tion, which reflects an age-old mortuary wish, leads up to the first direct equations of the deceased: first with Nun, and then with Re, his *ba*, and his cycle. The fact that Nun, the god of the primeval waters, is placed at the beginning corresponds to the high regard he also enjoys in the Book of the Heavenly Cow and to his active role at the end of the Book of Gates.

The ceiling text that follows invokes the United One and equates the deceased with the *ba* and the corpse of this god; it thus represents a high point of the book, not only because of the way it is inserted, but also be-cause of its content. A remark regarding recitation makes reference to the forms of the gods and to the offerings due them. The ensuing speech of the deceased king is addressed to them as the "gods who are in the West"; "I am one of you," he emphasizes, after which he again identifies himself with the sun god, with whom he shares the triumph "over all his enemies in the sky and on earth," and thus in the afterlife as a whole. There follows the brief fourth litany, "Jubilation to you," consisting of three double verses, wherein Osiris is also addressed; Re and Osiris greet and extend their hands to each other.

Through the power of his *ba*, Re dispels the darkness and allows the netherworld to see; the deceased also hopes for the renewal of his eyes and the return of his heart. With its eight double verses, the fifth litany, "You have commanded for me, as (for) Akhty," is a general evocation of the care of the god. A prayer follows for deliverance from the slaughterers in the netherworld, from their cauldrons, their traps, and their ovens, "for I am Re." In its fifteen double verses, the sixth litany follows a depiction of the majestic appearance of the god as *ba* with the request, "Oh Re, come to me, oh guide" and further identifications and dialogues with the "weary of heart" in the netherworld. An appearance of the pelican-goddess is inserted here; she is also represented at Abydos and is supposed to care for the deceased, who at the same time makes his appearance in all the splendor of the sun god.

The seventh litany, which is composed of five double verses ("Truly, you have caused me to ascend"), is followed by a deification of the limbs, by means of which the deceased becomes "entirely a god." There is an ensuing stress on an equation with Osiris, in which the deceased king also appears as the god's son and assumes command from him. In his double role as Re and Osiris, he turns to those who dwell in the hereafter, those who are "provided with offerings," and this section ends with the rejoicing of the eighth litany, "Hail, well led . . . ." The text concludes with a prayer to the realm of the dead as the "West" in the ninth litany and a final identification of the deceased king as Re; toward the end appears the old formula according to which the *ba* belongs to the sky and the corpse to the earth, with the additional phrase "among the gods."

The hours of the night play no role in this book, though the number twelve seems to be significant throughout.

87. Litany of Re, title illustration.
Drawing by A. Brodbeck.

88.   Litany of Re, figures from the Great Litany, right-hand row. Photo by A. Brodbeck.

89.   Litany of Re, figures from the Great Litany, right-hand row. Photo by A. Brodbeck.

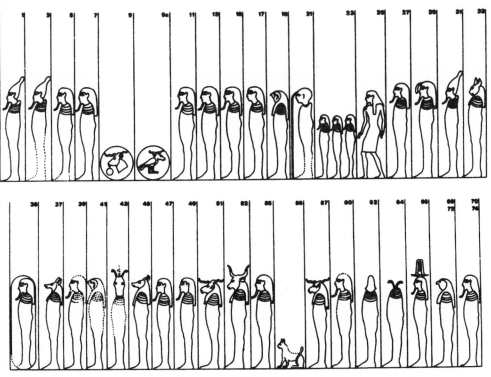

90. Litany of Re, figures of the Great Litany, left-hand row. Drawing by A. Brodbeck.

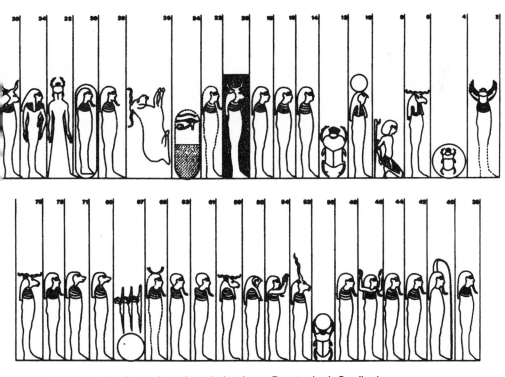

91. Litany of Re, figures from the right-hand row. Drawing by A. Brodbeck.

The Book of the Heavenly Cow
Sources

The Book of the Heavenly Cow is first attested on the outermost of the four gilded shrines (Shrine I) of Tutankhamun, though in incomplete form. Three more or less complete versions occur in the tombs of Sethos I, Ramesses II, and Ramesses III, each in a subsidiary room of the sarcophagus chamber reserved exclusively for this book. Ramesses VI included a brief excerpt in the left niche of the third corridor of his tomb, which has no subsidiary rooms, and an even briefer excerpt exists on a papyrus from the Ramesside Period now in Turin (Cat. 1982). The book was not used after the New Kingdom, though it was integrated into the Book of the Faiyum from the Roman Period and thus into the most important late myth of that region.

The continuation of the text on Tutankhamun's shrine ("words to be spoken by these deities who have gone off alive . . .") must also have been in the tomb of Sethos I, for traces of columns of text, which we did not include in our edition (see "Research" section), are still visible on the badly damaged left jamb of the entrance to subsidiary room M. Because of damage, it is no longer possible to determine where this excerpt ended or whether it was also present in other tombs.

Research

The striking representation of the heavenly cow in the tomb of Sethos I was copied by early visitors such as Henry Salt and Robert Hay. Edouard Naville published Sethos I's complete version in 1876, with a translation into French, and the version in the tomb of Ramesses III in 1885. He also supplied a first translation into English in 1876, while the first German translation was published by Heinrich Brugsch in 1881. Its parallel to the biblical narrative of the Flood has inspired great interest in the first part of the text, both within and outside Egyptology, and it has been translated often.

The first synoptic edition was published in 1941 by Charles Maystre, who was the first to take the version of Ramesses II into account, though he omitted that of Tutankhamun; this version was published by Alexandre Piankoff only in 1955, three decades after its discovery. After again checking and recording all the existing versions and securing once again the version of Ramesses III, which had been lost after Maystre (and also after A. Piankoff, *ASAE* 40, 1940: 289), Erik Hornung and colleagues

published an improved edition in 1983, which included a metrical translit-
eration by Gerhard Fecht; a second edition, with four pages of supple-
mental material and corrections, appeared in 1991.

Structure and Language

In Fecht's metrical structuring, the text has 330 verses, exactly half of
which are apportioned to the two parts of the text that occur before the
description of the representation. The language and orthography display some Late Egyptian influences, so that the book cannot have been
written long before it was first recorded under Tutankhamun. Aside
from the representation of the cow, there are no obvious breaks to allow
a clear structuring of the composition. Nevertheless, remarks inserted
into the text and other criteria permit a rough division into four parts. In
addition to the dominating figure of the cow of heaven, two further illustrations are inserted into the third part; they depict Neheh and Djet,
who are personifications of time, and the king supporting the sky.

Content

The central motif of the book is the rebellion of humankind against the
aged sun god, Re, and its punishment by the fiery "eye" of the god, the
goddess Hathor. This "fall" occasioned a total reordering of the world,
which had previously been in a golden age and was still little differenti-
ated: deities and humans alike were under the sovereignty of the sun
god, who had not yet begun his daily course through the sky and the
netherworld; the alternation of day and night was unknown, as were the
sky and the netherworld, for death did not yet exist. After Re consulted
with the primeval deities, and especially with Nun, Hathor was dispatched to inflict punishment. A part of humanity was annihilated, but
a portion remained whom the sun god saved from the fury of the goddess by causing her to become drunk on beer colored blood-red.

The reordering of the world consisted of Re's withdrawal to the sky
on the back of the celestial cow, which in the future would have to be
supported by Shu and the eight *Heh*-gods (figures 92 and 93), though
time (as Neheh and Djet; figure 94) and Pharaoh (figure 95) are also presented as supports of the sky. From his new location, Re concerned himself with establishing the netherworld, which was now necessary as a
realm for the dead; the third part of the book deals with this. The netherworld was populated with serpents, which were entrusted to the care of
the earth god Geb.

92. Book of the Heavenly Cow, the cow supported by Shu and the *Heh*-gods. From the tomb of Sethos I. Photo by H. Hauser.

93. Book of the Heavenly Cow, the cow supported by Shu and the *Heh*-gods. After A. Pi-ankoff, *The Shrines of Tut-Ankh-Amon* (New York, 1955), p. 142, fig. 46.

94. Book of the Heavenly Cow, *Neneh* (left) and *Djet* as supports of the sky. After Ch. Maystre, *BIFAO* 40 (1941): 114.

95. Book of the Heavenly Cow, Pharaoh as support of the sky. After Ch. Maystre, *BIFAO* 40 (1941): 113.

The fourth and last part of the book is devoted to the power of magic and contains the well-known theology of *ba*, according to which various deities and sacred animals are *ba*s of other divinities.

The first part places considerable emphasis on the royal role of the sun god: he bears the royal title, there is a cartouche around the name Re, and rulership over deities and humans is specifically attributed to him. This accounts for the importance of the text for Pharaoh, who was the "son" and successor of Re and who withdrew upon death to the sky, like Re on the back of the heavenly cow. As stated by the primeval god Nun, he was able to dwell in this afterlife in the sky "until the end of time."

The Book of Traversing Eternity

Sources

The preserved sources of the Book of Traversing Eternity stem overwhelmingly from the Roman Period, that is, the first and second centuries C.E. The origin of the book probably lay in the Ptolemaic Period, however, for two papyri in the Louvre (N 3166 and N 3284), two stelae (one in the Vatican and one in Cairo), and the sarcophagus lid of Imhotep belong to this period. A papyrus in Chicago is supposed to stem from Esna, but the other fifteen are probably all from Thebes, while the two stelae are from the delta or the Faiyum and the sarcophagus lid from Abydos. P. Leiden T 32, which is from the time of Nero (65 C.E.), and P. Vatican 55 supply a long version, whereas the remaining sources are more or less highly abridged.

Structure and Language

The modern designation of the texts follows the ancient title. The traversing (*zebeb*) is understood as the spending of a period of time—in this case all available time and also, analogously, the annual cycle of religious festivals. But since eternity (*neheh*) tends to be a synonym for afterlife, the expression remains ambiguous. Unlike the Books of the Netherworld, this guide to the afterlife (as many have considered it to be) is not thoroughly illustrated, though some papyri have vignettes or an introductory representation and a few depict the Judgment of the Dead from the Book of the Dead. The text is sometimes combined with texts from the Books of Breathing.

The book is composed in Middle Egyptian and written in hieratic, though the excerpts on stelae and on the sarcophagus lid are written in hieroglyphs. Formally, the text is arranged into couplets.

Content

As Assmann stresses in *LÄ* II (see the bibliography), the text has incorrectly been described as a guide to the afterlife and a survey of the regions of the hereafter. In actuality it describes the return of the deceased into the realm of the living, extensive visits to Egyptian sanctuaries, and participation in their rites and the traditions of their festivals, especially those of Osiris. Nevertheless, the book is intended for use after death, as a topographically arranged "festival calendar for the dead," as Assmann calls it. The deceased know that they are secure in an eternal community of celebrants, their existence in the afterlife bound to sacred places and times. They were also supposed to be able to move about freely in the hereafter and to have access to Osiris. As Akhenaten had already attempted in vain, the realm of the dead was brought into this life, and the this other-worldly Egypt became the "temple of the world," as it came to be viewed in late classical antiquity. Whether the text was also intended for cultic use is uncertain but definitely plausible. In one variant of the title, "Praying to the *akh* of NN," the text appears to be a hymn to the dead in the blessed *akh* form of existence.

GLOSSARY

The purpose of this glossary is to assist readers who are not familiar with Egyptian religion or the study of ancient Egypt more generally. A great deal more information about most of the deities mentioned in this volume can be found in Byron E. Shafer, ed., *Religion in Ancient Egypt: Gods, Myths, and Personal Practice* (Ithaca: Cornell University Press, 1991) and Dimitri Meeks and Christine Favard-Meeks, *Daily Life of the Egyptian Gods,* trans. G. M. Goshgarian (Ithaca: Cornell University Press, 1996).

Aker   A god of the earth; usually represented as a double sphinx.
Akh (pl. **akhu**)   Transfigured one; a designation of the deceased.
Akhty   "He of the horizon"; an epithet of Horus as a solar deity.
Amun   A god of Thebes who eventually became the chief god of Egypt.
Anubis   Jackal-headed god of mummification; sometimes depicted standing by the bier tending to the mummy.
Apophis   A god who, in the form of a serpent, tried each night to prevent the sun from rising and thus had to be defeated.
Aqen   An obscure god in the netherworld.
Astronomical ceiling   A ceiling in a tomb chamber decorated with depictions of the constellations of the nighttime sky.
Atum   A creator god; also, the evening form of the sun god.
Ba (pl. **bau**)   A sort of soul or manifestation of a deceased person or a deity.
Buchis bull   The sacred bull of the city of Armant.
Canopic chest   A chest fashioned to hold the jars containing the viscera of the deceased, which were removed during the mummification process.
Children of Horus   Gods who personified the four jars that contained the viscera of the deceased.

Cryptographic writing   A form of writing in which certain hieroglyphs are substituted for others, creating writings of words that are quite different from normal ones.

Decan   A star or group of stars representing a ten-day period of the year, which was divided into twelve months of thirty days each, plus five epagomenal (extra) days.

Demotic   A stage of the language and of the writing system that came into general use in Dynasty 26.

Duat   A designation of the netherworld.

Enigmatic writing   See **Cryptographic writing**.

Ennead   A group of nine deities; secondarily, a group of deities of any number.

Geb   A god of the earth.

Hathor   A goddess, sometimes represented as a cow, who could personify the sky.

Heka   God of magic.

Horus   Son of Osiris and Isis.

Hu   A god; personification of "authoritative utterance."

Isis   Sister/wife of Osiris and mother of Horus.

Ka   Life force.

Khentamentiu   "Foremost of the westerners"; a god of the dead at Abydos who was eventually identified with Osiris.

Khepri   A form of the sun, especially the rising sun; depicted as a scarab beetle.

Late Egyptian   A stage of the Egyptian language used in writing texts during late Dynasty 18 and the Ramesside Period.

Maat   Goddess of truth and cosmic order.

Mehen   A serpent; often depicted as a many-coiled serpent protecting the sun god in the netherworld.

Mekhentienirty   A god identified with Horus; could be depicted as a mongoose.

Middle Egyptian   A stage of the Egyptian language that took form in the Middle Kingdom and remained the classical language for the remainder of the history of pharaonic civilization.

Neith   Goddess of Sais. Also the name of a queen of Pepy II.

Nephthys   Sister of Isis, Osiris, and Seth; often depicted together with Isis, either mourning Osiris or keeping the sun disk in motion.

NN.   Stands for the name of a person; see **Osiris NN.**

Nome   One of the administrative/geographical districts, or provinces, into which Egypt was divided.

Nun   A god who personified the primeval water that preceded creation and was believed to surround the created cosmos.

Nut   Goddess of the sky.

Old Egyptian   A stage of the Egyptian language in use during the Old Kingdom.

Orion   A constellation identified by the Egyptians with the god Osiris.

Osireion   The cenotaph (false tomb) of Sethos I at Abydos.

Osiris   God of the dead and ruler of the netherworld.

Osiris NN   The name of Osiris, used as an epithet, followed by the name of an individual.

Ouroboros   A serpent depicted biting its own tail.

Penwenti   A crocodile in the netherworld that might represent the primeval waters out of which the sun rises in the morning.

Ptah   A creator god worshiped at Memphis.
Re   The sun god.
Sakhmet   A lion-headed goddess of healing.
Shetit   A name of the realm of the dead.
Shu   God of air and light.
Sia   God of perception and spokesman of Re.
Sokar   A god of the dead.
Tatenen   God of the depths of the earth.
Tayt   A goddess in the netherworld.
Tefnut   A goddess; sister of Shu.
Thoth   God of Hermopolis; sometimes represented as a baboon and sometimes as an ibis.
Uraeus (pl. **uraei**)   Cobra.
Vignette   A symbolic representation summarizing the intent or content of a text.
Vizier   The official who headed the royal administration.

BIBLIOGRAPHY

Abbreviations

ÄAT	Ägypten und Altes Testament
ADAIK	Abhandlungen des Deutschen Archäologischen Instituts Kairo
ÄgAbh	Ägyptologische Abhandlungen
AH	Aegyptiaca Helvetica
AnAeg	Analecta Aegyptiaca
AnOr	Analecta Orientalia
ASAE	*Annales du Service des Antiquités de l'Égypte*
ASAW	Abhandlungen der sächsischen Akademie der Wissenschaften zu Leipzig, Philologisch-historische Klasse
ASP	*American Studies in Papyrology*
AVDAIK	Archäologische Veröffentlichungen des Deutschen Archäologischen Instituts Kairo
BÄBA	Beiträge zur ägyptischen Beuforschung und Altertumskunde
BACE	*Bulletin of the Australian Centre for Egyptology*
BAe	Bibliotheca Aegyptiaca
BE	Bibliothèque d'Étude
BES	Brown Egyptological Studies
BG	Bibliothèque Générale
BIFAO	*Bulletin de l'Institut Français d'Archéologie Orientale au Caire*
BO	*Bibliotheca Orientalis*
BSEG	*Bulletin de la Société d'Égyptologie, Genève*
BSFE	*Bulletin de la Société Française d'Égyptologie*
CdE	*Chronique d'Égypte*

CRIPEL Cahier de Recherches de l'Institut de Papyrologie et d'Égyptologie de Lille

DAWBIO Deutsche Akademie der Wissenschaften zu Berlin, Institut für Orientforschung, Veröffentlichung

DE *Discussions in Egyptology*

DVS Danske Videnskabernas Selskab, Historisk-filologiske Skrifter

EMAE Études de Mythologie et d'Archéologie Égyptiennes

ET *Études et travaux*

EVO *Egitto e Vicino Oriente*

GM *Göttinger Miszellen*

GO Göttinger Orientforschungen, IV. Reihe, Ägypten

HÄB Hildesheimer ägyptologische Beiträge

JARCE *Journal of the American Research Center in Egypt*

JEA *Journal of Egyptian Archaeology*

JEOL *Jaarbericht van het Vooraziatisch-Egyptisch Genootschap "Ex Oriente Lux"*

JNES *Journal of Near Eastern Studies*

JSSEA *Journal of the Society for the Study of Egyptian Antiquities*

LA Liber Annuus, Studii Biblici Franciscani (Jerusalem)

LÄ Wolfgang Helck and Eberhard Otto (eds.), *Lexikon der Ägyptologie*, 6 vols. (Wiesbaden, 1975-1992)

LAe *Lingua Aegyptia*

MAIBL n.s. Mémoires de l'Académie des Inscriptions et Belles-Lettres, nouvelle série

MÄS Münchner Ägyptologische Studien

MÄU Münchner Ägyptologische Untersuchungen

MDAIK *Mitteilungen des Deutschen Archäologischen Instituts, Abteilung Kairo*

MEES Memoir of the Egypt Exploration Society

MIFAO Mémoires publiés par les membres de l'Institut Français d'Archéologie Orientale du Caire

MVVEG Mededelingen en verhandelingen van het Vooraziatisch-Egyptisch Genootschap "Ex Oriente Lux"

NAWG Nachrichten der Akademie der Wissenschaften in Göttingen, I. Philologisch-historische Klasse

OA *Oriens Antiquus*

OBO Orbis Biblicus et Orientalis

OCE Oxfordshire Communications in Egyptology

OIP Oriental Institute Publications

OLA Orientalia Lovaniensia Analecta

PSBA *Proceedings of the Society of Biblical Archaeology*

PTA Papyrologische Texte und Abhandlungen

RdE *Revue d'Égyptologie*

RHR	*Revue de l'Histoire des Religions*
RT	*Receuil de Travaux relatifs à la philologie et à l'archéologie égyptiennes et assyriennes*
SAGA	Studien zur Archäologie und Geschichte Altägyptens
SAK	*Studien zur altägyptischen Kultur*
SAOC	Studies in Ancient Oriental Civilization
SHR	Studies in the History of Religions
SSN	Studia Semitica Neerlandica
TL	*Theologische Literaturzeitung*
TSBA	*Transactions of the Society of Biblical Archaeology*
UCBUCP	University of California, Berkeley, University of California Publications, Near Eastern Studies
UGAAe	Untersuchungen zur Geschichte und Altertumskunde Aegyptens
VA	*Varia Aegyptiaca*
WZKM	*Wiener Zeitschrift für die Kunde des Morgenlandes*
YES	Yale Egyptological Studies
ZÄS	*Zeitschrift für ägyptische Sprache und Altertumskunde*
ZDMG	*Zeitschrift der Deutschen Morgenländischen Gesellschaft*

Introduction

For Jean-François Champollion's letters from Egypt, see *Lettres écrites d'Égypte et de Nubie en 1828 et 1829* (Paris, 1833). On the mortuary liturgies, see J. Assmann in S. Israelit-Groll, ed., *Studies in Egyptology Presented to Miriam Lichtheim* (Jerusalem, 1990), 1: 1–45, and *LÄ*, 6, cols. 998–1006, *s.v.* "Verklärung."

The Pyramid Texts

A first report regarding their discovery was published by H. Brugsch, *ZÄS* 19 (1881): 1-15, and the first text edition by G. Maspero in several articles in *RT*; the first article appeared in vol. 3 (1882), and the last in vol. 14 (1893). Shortly thereafter, the series of articles was reprinted as G. Maspero, *Les inscriptions des Pyramides de Saqqarah* (Paris, 1894). Beginning in 1908, K. Sethe published his still definitive edition, *Die altägyptische Pyramidentexte* (Leipzig, 1908-1922; rpt. Darmstadt, 1960), which is supplemented by G. Jéquier's publications of the material found by him at Saqqara South: *Fouilles à Saqqarah: La pyramide d'Oudjebten* (Cairo, 1928); *Fouilles à Saqaqarah: Les pyramides des reines Neit et Apouit* (Cairo, 1933); *La pyramide d'Aba* (Cairo, 1935); *Fouilles à Saqqarah: Le monument funéraire de Pepi II*, vol. 1 (Cairo, 1936). J. Leclant has supplied a whole series of preliminary notices of more recent work; by way of an interim report, see his surveys in *L'égyptologie en 1979*, vol. 2 (Paris, 1982), pp. 31–35, as well as at subsequent international congresses and in the journal *Orientalia*, under the title "Fouilles et travaux en Égypte et au Soudan."

Only after K. Sethe's death did his six-volume *Übersetzung und Kommentar zu den altägyptischen Pyramidentexten* (Glückstadt, 1935–1962) appear; this work covers spells 213–582. Further translations were published by L. Speleers, *Traduction, index, et vocabulaire des textes des pyramides égyptiennes* (Brussels, 1924; rev. ed. 1934); S. A. B. Mercer, *The Pyramid Texts in Translation and Commentary*, 4 vols. (New York, 1952); and R. O. Faulkner, *The Ancient Egyptian Pyramid Texts*, 2 vols. (Oxford, 1969); Faulkner's second volume contains material supplementary to Sethe's text edition, and see also the improvements by E. Edel, *OLZ* 69 (1974): 131–137 and *ZÄS* 102 (1975): 31–36. A small selection of texts is to be found in M. Clagett, *Ancient Egyptian Science: A Source Book*, vol. 1 (Philadelphia, 1989), pp. 413–424, and a larger selection in S. Donadoni, *Testi religiosi egizi* (Turin, 1970), pp. 37–168. On Sethe's edition, see also H. Grapow, *ZDMG* 91 (1937): 537–554, with a French translation in *CdE* 14 (1939) 218–231. An index of citations was first published in 1971 by C. Crozier-Brelot as *Textes des Pyramides: Index des citations* (Paris, 1971), and since 1976, there have been several revised editions. In his translation volume, Faulkner supplies helpful indexes of deities and localities mentioned in the spells, though we still lack a glossary of the Pyramid Texts.

For discussion of the burial ritual, see S. Schott, *Bemerkungen zum ägyptischen Pyramidenkult*, Beiträge zur ägyptischen Bauforschung und Altertumskunde 5/2 (Cairo, 1950) and the critique by H. Bonnet, *JNES* 12 (1953): 257–273; J. Spiegel, *Das Auferstehungsritual der Unas-Pyramide*, ÄgAbh 23 (Wiesbaden, 1971); J. Spiegel, *ASAE* 53 (1956): 339–439; H. Altenmüller, *Die Texte zum Begräbnisritual in den Pyramiden des Alten Reiches*, ÄgAbh 24 (Wiesbaden, 1972); idem, *LÄ* V, cols. 14–16; W. Barta, *Die Bedeutung der Pyramidentexte für den verstorbenen König*, MÄS 39 (Berlin, 1981); J. Osing, *MDAIK* 42 (1986): 131–144; J. P. Allen, in C. Berger, G. Clerc, and N. Grimal, eds., *Hommages à Jean Leclant*, vol. 1 (Cairo, 1994), pp. 5–28; G. Englund, in ibid., pp. 169–180.

There are good photographs of Wenis's version in A. Piankoff, *The Pyramid of Unas*, Bollingen Series 40/5 (Princeton, 1968); samples from Teti in *Orientalia* 35 (1966), plates VIII–X, *BSFE* 46 (1966), plates II–IV, and J. Leclant and C. Berger in *Études sur l'Ancien Empire et la nécropole de Saqqara dédiées à J.-Ph. Lauer* (Montpellier, 1997), pp. 271–277; views of the sarcophagus chambers of Pepy I and Merenre in C. Aldred et al., *Le temps des Pyramides* (Paris, 1978), pp. 98–99, and Pepy I also in *Orientalia* 37 (1968): plates 22–24, 38 (1969), plates 22–25, and 39 (1970), plates 34–37; for Pepy II, see J. Leipoldt and S. Morenz, *Heilige Schriften: Beobachtungen zur Religionsgeschichte der antiken Mittelmeerwelt* (Leipzig, 1953), fig. 2; for the versions of Iput and Udjebten, see J. P. Allen, *JARCE* 23 (1986): 1–25.

The fundamental source for the later occurrences of the Pyramid Texts remains T. G. Allen, *Occurrences of Pyramid Texts with Cross Indexes of These and Other Egyptian Mortuary Texts*, SAOC 27 (Chicago, 1950). For the textual tradition of some of the spells, see J. Kahl, *Steh auf, gib Horus deine Hand* (Wiesbaden, 1996).

Middle Kingdom: W. C. Hayes, *The Texts in the Mastaba of Se'n-wosret-'nkh at Lisht* (New York, 1937), and on the relationship of this version to the texts of Wenis on the example of spells 302–312, see J. Kahl, *SAK* 22 (1995): 195–209; L. H. Lesko, *Index of the Spells on Egyptian Middle Kingdom Coffins and Related Documents* (Berkeley, 1979); W. Barta, *ZÄS* 113 (1986): 1–8; and idem, *GM* 120 (1991): 7–12. On the

Pyramid Texts on canopic chests of this period, see B. Lüscher, *Untersuchungen zu ägyptischen Kanopenkästen vom Alten Reich bis zum Ende der Zweiten Zwischenzeit*, HÄB 31 (Hildesheim, 1990), pp. 66–71.

New Kingdom: W. C. Hayes, *Royal Sarcophagi of the XVII. Dynasty* (Princeton, 1935). Late Period: For Dynasty 26, a rather large work by P. de Smet is expected, and see also M. Patanè, *BSEG* 16 (1992): 65–67, on the most frequently attested spells, and C. E. Sander-Hansen, *Die religiösen Texte auf dem Sarg der Anchnesneferibre, neu herausgegeben und erklärt* (Copenhagen, 1937). For the tombs at Saqqara, see E. Bresciani, S. Pernigotti, and M. P. Giangeri Silvis, *La tomba di Ciennehebu* (Pisa, 1977), pp. 25–40; for an early Ptolemaic version on papyrus, see G. Möller, *Über die in einem späthieratischen Papyrus des Berliner Museums erhaltenen Pyramidentexte* (Berlin, 1900). For an adoption in the Ptolemaic temple of Edfu, see A. Grimm, *GM* 31 (1979): 35–46. For the Roman Period, see A. Szczudlowska, *ZÄS* 99 (1973): 25–29.

Orthography and grammar: On suppression and modification of signs, see P. Lacau, *ZÄS* 51 (1914): 1–64; on graphic dissimilations, see E. Drioton, *ASAE* 49 (1949): 57–68; O. Firchow, *Grundzüge der Stilistik in den altägyptischen Pyramidentexten*, DAWBIO 21 (Berlin, 1953); C. E. Sander-Hansen, *Studien zur Grammatik der Pyramidentexte*, AnAeg 6 (Copenhagen, 1956); E. Edel, *Altägyptische Grammatik*, 2 vols., AnOr 34 and 39 (Rome, 1955 and 1964), §§ 12–14; J. P. Allen, *The Inflection of the Verb in the Pyramid Texts*, BAe 2 (Malibu, 1984); J. Kahl, *LAe* 2 (1992): 99–116.

With regard to studies of the content of the texts, only a selection can be given here. Various themes are treated in the Excurses in vol. 4 of Mercer, *The Pyramid Texts* (see above). G. van der Leeuw, *Godsvoorstellingen in de oudaegyptische Pyramidetexten* (Leiden, 1916); Th. G. Allen, *Horus in the Pyramid Texts* (Chicago, 1916); J. Sainte Fare Garnot, *L'hommage aux dieux sous l'Ancien Empire égyptien d'après les Textes des Pyramides* (Paris, 1954); On prayers, see L. J. Cazemier, *JEOL* 15 (1957/58): 47–65. On the solar eye, see R. Anthes, *ZÄS* 86 (1961): 1–21. On the king and the star religion, see R. O. Faulkner, *JNES* 25 (1966): 153–161. On the ascension myth, see W. M. Davis, *JNES* 36 (1977): 161–179. On spiritual concepts, see K. Koch, *SAK* 11 (1984): 425–454; and Ch. Jacq, *Le Voyage dans l'autre monde selon l'Égypte ancienne* (Monaco, 1986). On divine conflicts, see V. A. Tobin, *JARCE* 30 (1993): 93–110. On themes and motifs, see H. Roeder, *LAe* 3 (1993):81–119. On the Duat, see N. Beaux, *BIFAO* 94 (1994): 1–6. O. Sirius and the young Horus, see idem, in C. Berger, G. Clerc, and N. Grimal, eds., *Hommages à Jean Leclant* (Cairo, 1994), vol. 1, pp. 61–72. Not yet published is R. Krauss, *Astronomische Konzepte und Jenseitsvorstellungen in den Pyramidentexten.*

Treatments of individual spells: Spell 263 (the reed float), W. Barta, *SAK* 2 (1975): 39–48 and H. Altenmüller, in *Hommages à François Daumas* (Montpellier, 1986), vol. 1, pp. 1–15; on the Cannibal Hymn, see H. Altenmüller, in J. Assmann, E. Feucht, and R. Grieshammer, eds., *Fragen an die altägyptische Literatur: Studien zum Gedenken an E. Otto* (Wiesbaden, 1977), pp. 19–39; on spell 23, J. Assmann, in C. Berger, G. Clerc, and N. Grimal, eds., *Hommages à Jean Leclant*, vol. 1 (Cairo, 1994), pp. 45–59; on spell 534, see J. Osing, ibid., pp. 279–284; on spell 659, see M. Heerma van Voss, ibid., pp. 217–220; and Ch. Leitz, *Orientalia* 65 (1996): 381–427 (spells against serpents).

Varia: On the discovery of the Pyramid Texts, see R. T. Ridley, *ZÄS* 110 (1983): 74–80; various further contributions in vol. 1 of C. Berger, G. Clerc, and N. Grimal, eds., *Hommages à Jean Leclant* (Cairo, 1994). In clear contrast to the Book of the Dead, the Pyramid Texts have had scant influence beyond the boundaries of Egyptology, notwithstanding the high regard in which scholars hold them. This is perhaps because of the difficulty of the texts and of the lack of translations and commentaries that could introduce their content to a wider public.

The Coffin Texts

The basic text publication is A. de Buck, *The Egyptian Coffin Texts*, 7 vols., OIP 34, 49, 64, 67, 73, 81, 87 (Chicago, 1935–1961). In his translation (see below), P. Barguet draws attention (p. 12) to some coffins that de Buck did not take into account. Still more material has been published by J. Vandier, "Deux textes religieux du Moyen Empire," in W. Helck, ed., *Festschrift für Siegfried Schott zu seinem 70. Geburtstag* (Wiesbaden, 1968), 121–124; A. Roccati, *OA* 13 (1974): 161–197 (Herakleopolis); G. Lapp, *Särge Des Mittleren Reiches aus der ehemaligen Sammlung Khashaba*, ÄgAbh 43 (Wiesbaden, 1985; Asyut); idem, *SAK* 13 (1986):135–145 (Asyut?); D. P. Silverman, in S. Israelit-Groll, ed., *Studies in Egyptology Presented to Miriam Lichtheim*, vol. 2 (Jerusalem, 1990), pp. 853–876 (Kom el-Hisn).

For early evaluations of the material, see J. H. Breasted, *Development of Religion and Thought in Ancient Egypt* (New York, 1912) and H. Kees, *Totenglauben und Jenseitsvorstellungen der alten Ägypter* (Berlin, 1926; 2d ed., Berlin, 1956). On the floor of the coffin of Sen, see H. Schack-Schackenburg, *Das Buch von den zwei Wegen des seligen Toten* (Leipzig, 1903).

On the textual tradition in the New Kingdom, see D. P. Silverman, *L'Égyptologie en 1979: Axes prioritaires de recherches*, vol. 1 (Paris, 1982), pp. 67–70 (spell 902); on the Late Period, see G. Soukiassian, ibid., vol. 2, pp. 55–61; L. Gestermann, *SAK* 19 (1992): 117–132; A. el-Sawi and F. Gomaà, *Das Grab des Panehsi, Gottesvaters von Heliopolis in Matariya*, ÄAT 23 (Wiesbaden, 1993); H. Guksch, *Die Gräber des Nacht-Min und des Men-cheper-Ra-seneb, Theben Nr. 87 und 79*, AVAIK 34 (Mainz, 1995), pp. 74–75.

Translations of the entire corpus have been published by R. O. Faulkner, *The Ancient Egyptian Coffin Texts*, 3 vols. (Warminster, 1973–1978; rpt. 1994) and P. Barguet, *Les textes des sarcophages égyptiens du Moyen Empire* (Paris, 1986), with bibliography. Small selections of texts are translated by S. Donadoni, *Testi religiosi egizi* (Turin, 1970), pp. 195–212 and M. Clagett, *Ancient Egyptian Science: A Source Book*, vol. 1 (Philadelphia, 1989), pp. 437–443. On the distribution of the spells on the coffins, see L. H. Lesko, *Index of the Spells on Egyptian Middle Kingdom Coffins and Related Documents* (Berkeley, 1979). A survey of the secondary literature was published by R. Grieshammer, *Die altägptischen Sargtexte in der Forschung seit 1936*, ÄgAbh 28 (Wiesbaden, 1974); see further M. Crozier, *Textes des sarcophages: Index des citations* (Paris, 1971). A dating of the coffins on the basis of typology was attempted by H. Willems, *Chests of Life: A Study of the Typology and Conceptual Development of Middle Kingdom Standard Class Coffins*, MVVEG 25 (Leiden, 1988) and G. Lapp, *Typologie der Särge und Sargkammern von der 6. bis 13. Dynastie*, SAGA 7 (Heidelberg, 1993); on a distribution by linguistic criteria, see already W. Schenkel,

Frühmittelägyptische Studien (Bonn, 1962). On the use of spells on canopic chests, see B. Lüscher, *Untersuchungen zu ägyptischen Kanopenkästen vom Alten Reich bis zum Ende der Zweiten Zwischenzeit*, HÄB 31 (Hildesheim, 1990), pp. 71–76.

Publications of individual coffins: G. Maspero, *Trois années de fouilles* (Paris, 1885; Harhotpe); S. Birch, *Egyptian Texts of the Earliest Period from the Coffin of Amamu in the British Museum* (London, 1886; el-Bersha); G. Steindorff, *Grabfunde des Mittleren Reiches in den Königlichen Museen zu Berlin*, vol. 2 (Berlin, 1901; coffin of Sebk-o from Gebelein); H. Schäfer, *Priestergräber und andere Grabfunde vom Ende des Alten Reiches bis zur griechischen Zeit vom Totentempel des Ne-user-rê* (Leipzig, 1908; Abusir); E.L.B. Terrace, *Egyptian Paintings of the Middle Kingdom: The Tomb of Djehuty-nekht* (New York, 1968; el-Bersha, incomplete); and H. Willems, *The Coffin of Heqata* (Leuven, 1996). On the coffins in Cairo, see the *Catalogue générale* volumes by P. Lacau, *Sarcophages antérieurs au Nouvel Empire*, 2 vols. (Cairo, 1904 and 1906).

For a collection of vignettes, see P. Eschweiler, *Bildzauber im alten Ägypten: Die Verwendung von Bildern und Gegenständen in magischen Handlungen nach den Texten des Mittleren und Neuen Reiches*, OBO 137 (Freiburg and Göttingen, 1994), p. 161, n. 2 (see also ibid., p. 187). For a concordance of one of the spells, see R. Gundlach and W. Schenkel, *Lexikalisch-grammatische Liste zu Spruch 335a der altägypt. Sargtexte*, 2 vols. (Darmstadt, 1970); on the continuation of this project, see W. Schenkel, *Aus der Arbeit an einer Konkordanz zu den altägyptischen Sargtexten*, GO 12 (Wiesbaden, 1983) and idem, *ZÄS* 121 (1994): 142–153; further, P. Jürgens, *GM* 105 (1988): 27–34, and idem, *Grundlinien einer Überlieferungsgeschichte der altägyptischen Sargtexte: Stemmata und Archetypen der Spruchgruppen 30–32 + 33–37, 75(–83), 162 + 164, 225 + 226 und 343 + 345*, GO 31 (Wiesbaden, 1995). Specific sequences of spells have been worked out by G. Lapp, *SAK* 16 (1989): 171–202 and *SAK* 17 (1990): 221–234. There is a complete lexical analysis of de Buck's edition in Leiden; this index is not yet available in print, though it can be accessed via the Internet. P. Barguet appended an index of divine names and place names, as well as some "notabilia," to his translation. A grammar of Middle Egyptian based heavily on the Coffin Texts was written by D. Müller, *A Concise Introduction to Middle Egyptian* (Lethbridge, 1975; privately distributed).

On the Book of the Two Ways, in each case with full translations, see A. Piankoff, *Wanderings of the Soul*, Bollingen Series 40/6 (New York, 1974); L. H. Lesko, *The Ancient Egyptian Book of Two Ways*, UCBUCP 17 (Berkeley, 1972); and E. Hermsen, *Die zwei Wege des Jenseits*, OBO 112 (Freiburg and Göttingen, 1991), with a helpful review by W. Waitkus, *BO* 53 (1996): 666–674. Relationships between the Book of the Two Ways and the Book of the Dead were pointed out by H. Grapow, *ZÄS* 46 (1909): 77–81, and relationships with the Amduat by idem, *ZÄS* 72 (1936): 12–39. The regions of the hereafter are represented on a coffin from Gebelein, now in Turin (de Buck, *Coffin Texts* 6, p. 271); on this and a possible connection with the last tale of Papyrus Westcar, see E. Hornung, *ZÄS* 100 (1973): 33–35. P. Barguet has attempted to explain the Book of the Two Ways as an initiatory text and to connect it with the plan of a temple; see *RdE* 21 (1969): 7–17.

A first collection of coffin lids from Asyut with decans and other stars was made by A. Pogo, *Isis* 17 (1932): 6–24, and a more complete one (twelve coffins) by O. Neugebauer and R. A. Parker, *Egyptian Astronomical Texts*, vol. 1: *The Early Decans*, BES 3 (Providence, 1960); on other diagonal star clocks, see J. Kahl, *SAK* 20

(1993): 95, with references, and for text criticism, see ibid., pp. 95–107. For an explanation of the astronomy, see M. Schramm, in E. Brunner-Traut and H. Brunner, eds., *Die Ägyptische Sammlung der Universität Tübingen* (Mainz, 1981), pp. 219–227 and Ch. Leitz, *Altägyptische Sternuhren*, OLA 62 (Leuven, 1995).

On individual spells and sequences of spells: H. Kees, *Göttinger Totenbuchstudien*, UGAAe 17 (Berlin, 1954; spell 227/228); R. O. Faulkner, *JEA* 48 (1962): 36–44 (spells 38–40); M. Heerma van Voss, *De oudste versie van Dodenboek 17a: Coffin Texts spreuk 335a* (Leiden, 1963; spell 335); J. Zandee, *ZÄS* 97 (1971) to 101 (1974; spells 75–81); L. H. Lesko, *JARCE* 9 (1971/72): 89–110 (spells 464–466); R. O. Faulkner, *JEA* 58 (1972): 91–94 (spell 313); D. Müller, *JEA* 58 (1972): 99–125 (spell 404); R. Sayed, *RdE* 26 (1974):73–82 (spells 407–408); D. Bidoli, *Die Sprüche der Fangnetze in den altägyptischen Sargtexten*, ADAIK 9 (Glückstadt, 1976; spells 473–480); J. Zandee, in J. Assmann, E. Feucht, and R. Grieshammer, eds., *Fragen an die altägyptische Literatur: Studien zum Gedenken an E. Otto* (Wiesbaden, 1977), pp. 511–529 (spells 355, 362, and others); A. Niccacci, *LA* 28 (1978): 5–23 (spell 76); G. E. Kadish, *JSSEA* 9 (1978/79): 203–217 (on the theme of eating excrement); V. A. Tobin, in S. Israelit-Groll, ed., *Papers for Discussion*, vol. 1 (Jerusalem, 1982), pp. 166–190 (spell 573); J. Zandee, *BO* 41 (1984): 5–33 (spell 173); J. Assmann, *Ägypten: Theologie und Frömmigkeit einer frühen Hochkultur* (Stuttgart, 1984), pp. 204–221 (spells 1130 and 80); M. Heerma van Voss, in L. H. Lesko, ed., *Egyptological Studies in Honor of R. A. Parker Presented on the Occasion of His 78th Birthday, December 10, 1983* (Hanover, 1986), pp. 49–52 (spell 106); J. F. Borghouts, in J. H. Kamstra, H. Milde, and K. Wagtendonk, eds., *Funerary Symbols and Religion: Essays Dedicated to Professor M. S. H. G. Heerma van Voss on the Occasion of His Retirement from the Chair of the History of Ancient Religions at the University of Amsterdam* (Kampen, 1988), pp. 12–22 (spell 336); J. Zandee, ibid., pp. 165–182 (spells 363–366); H. Buchberger, *Transformation und Transformat: Sargtextstudien I*, ÄgAbh 52 (Wiesbaden, 1993; the transformation spells); S. Bickel, in C. Berger, G. Clerc, and N. Grimal, eds., *Hommages à Jean Leclant*, vol. 1 (Cairo, 1994), pp. 81–97 (spell 80); A. de Jong, *SAK* 21 (1994): 141–157 (spell 38).

The most extensive treatment of the content remains that of H. Kees, *Totenglauben und Jenseitsvorstellungen der alten Ägypter*, 2d ed. (Berlin, 1956), though there is as yet no comprehensive account of beliefs regarding the afterlife in the Coffin Texts. On individual topics: On the *ba* in spells 99–104, E. Otto, in *Miscellanea Gregoriana* (Rome, 1941), pp. 151–160; on the Isle of Fire, H. Kees, *ZÄS* 78 (1942): 41–53; on a teaching about the world of nature, S. Morenz, *WZKM* 54 (1957): 119–129; on concepts of punishment, J. Zandee, *Death as an Enemy According to Egyptian Conceptions*, SHR 5 (Leiden, 1960); on the Judgment of the Dead, R. Grieshammer, *Das Jenseitsgericht in den Sargtexten*, ÄgAbh 20 (Wiesbaden, 1970); on the Field of Offerings, L. H. Lesko, *JARCE* 9 (1971/72): 89–101; B. Altenmüller, *Synkretismus in den Sargtexten*, GO 7 (Wiesbaden, 1975); on the spells for having water at one's disposal, J. Zandee, *JEOL* 24 (1976): 1–47; on the motif of eating excrement, idem, *BO* 41 (1984): 5–33 and G. E. Kadish, *JSSEA* 9 (1978/79): 203–217; on traveling through the hereafter, Ch. Jacq, *L. Voyage dans l'autre monde selon l'Égypte ancienne* (Monaco, 1986); on concepts regarding creation, S. Bickel, *La cosmogonie égyptienne avant le Nouvel Empire*, OBO 134 (Freiburg and Göttingen, 1994); on the Lake of Fire, E. Hermsen, in T. DuQuesne, ed., *Hermes Aegyptiacus: Egyptological Studies for B. H. Stricker* (Oxford, 1995), pp. 73–86.

The Book of the Dead

The basic publication is still E. Naville, *Das Aegyptische Todtenbuch der XVIII. bis XX. Dynastie aus verschiedenen Urkunden zusammengestellt* (Berlin, 1886; rpt. Graz, 1971). It ends with spell 186; spells 187–190 were added by E. A. W. Budge in his edition in hieroglyphic type, *The Book of the Dead: The Chapters of Coming Forth by Day* (London, 1898 and many later editions). While Naville gives only spells from the New Kingdom textual tradition, Budge aimed for comprehensiveness and included spells from a variety of periods. On the early attestations, see I. Franco, *BIFAO* 88 (1988): 71–82 (mummy shrouds), as well as R. Parkinson and St. Quirke, in A. B. Lloyd, ed., *Studies in Pharaonic Religion and Society in Honor of J. Gwyn Griffiths* (London, 1992), pp. 37–51; on their employment on royal grave goods, see H. Beinlich, *GM* 102 (1988): 7–18; on their use in the decoration of royal tombs, see F. Abitz, *Pharao als Gott in den Unterweltsbüchern des Neuen Reiches*, OBO 146 (Freiburg and Göttingen, 1995), pp. 174–199. On occurrences on tomb walls, see M. Saleh, *Das Totenbuch in den thebanischen Beamtengräbern des Neuen Reiches: Texte und Vignetten*, AVDAIK 40 (Mainz, 1984); on ostraca, see M. Heerma van Voss, *Phoenix* 14 (1968): 165–171; on scarabs, see M. Malaise, *Les scarabées du coeur dans l'Égypte ancienne* (Brussels, 1978). Many Books of the Dead, with bibliographical information, are listed in M. Bellion, *Catalogue des manuscrits hiéroglyphiques et hiératiques et des dessins, sur papyrus, cuir ou tissu, publiés ou signalés* (Paris, 1987), with a list of individual spells on pp. 410–481.

Editions of manuscripts in museums: Chicago: T. G. Allen, *The Egyptian Book of the Dead: Documents in The Oriental Institute Museum at The University of Chicago* (Chicago, 1960). Cairo: I. Munro, *Die Totenbuch-Handschriften der 18. Dynastie im Ägyptischen Museum Cairo* (Wiesbaden, 1994). London: A. W. Shorter, *Catalogue of Egyptian Religious Papyri in the British Museum: Copies of the Book PR(T)-M-HRW from the XVIIIth to the XXIInd Dynasty* (London, 1938; partial, only to spell 17). Vatican: A. Gasse, *Les papyrus hiératiques et hiéroglyphiques du Museo Gregoriano Egizio* (Vatican City, 1993).

Editions of manuscripts, by period
Dynasty 18: General, taking into consideration eighty-five textual witnesses from this dynasty, I. Munro, *Untersuchungen zu den Totenbuch-Papyri der 18. Dynastie; Kriterien ihrer Datierung* (London, 1988) (and see A. Niwiński, *JEA* 77 [1991]: 212–215 and U. Luft, *BO* 48 [1991]: 90–93); idem, *GM* 116 (1990): 73–89 (Useramun); *Photographs of the Papyrus of Nebseni in the British Museum* (London, 1876); C. Leemans, *Aegyptische hieroglyphische lijkpapyrus (T. 2) van het Nederlandsche Museum van Oudheden te Leyden* (Leiden, 1882; Qenna); E. Naville, *The Funeral Papyrus of Iouiya* (London, 1908); E. Schiaparelli, *La tomba intatta dell'architetto Cha nella necropoli di Tebe* (Turin, 1927); T. Andrzejewski, *Ksiega umarlych piastunki Kai* (Warsaw, 1951); S. Ratié, *L. Papyrus de Neferoubenef* (Cairo, 1968); G. Thausing and T. Kerszt-Kratschmann, *Das grosse ägyptische Totenbuch (Papyrus Reinisch) der Papyrussammlung der Österreichischen Nationalbibliothek* (Cairo, 1969); P. Ronsacco, *Due Libri dei Morti del principio del Nuovo Regno* (Turin, 1996); I. Munro, *Das Totenbuch des Iah-Mes (p Louvre E. 11085) aus der frühen 18. Dyn.* (Wiesbaden, 1995); I. Munro, *Das Totenbuch des Bak-su (pKM1970.37/pBrocklehurst) aus der Zeit Amenophis' II.* (Wiesbaden,

1995); G. Lapp, *The Papyrus of Nu (BM EA 10477)* (London, 1997). The texts from the tomb of Senenmut can now be found in P. F. Dorman, *Tombs of Senenmut,* (New York, 1991).

Ramesside Period: Th. Dévéria, *Le Papyrus de Neb-Qed* (Paris, 1872); the same papyrus is also reproduced in the catalogue *Naissance de l'écriture* (Paris, 1982), pp. 288–291, while according to I. Munro, it dates to Dynasty 18; E. A. W. Budge, *The Book of the Dead: Facsimiles of the Papyri of Hunefer, Anhai, Kerasher and Netchemet with Supplementary Text from the Papyrus of Nu* (London, 1899); the papyri of Hunefer and Anhai also published by E. Rossiter, *Die ägyptischen Totenbücher* (Freiburg, 1984); L. Speleers, *L. Papyrus de Nefer Renpet* (Brussels, 1917; on the vignettes, see also the cited work by H. Milde, 1991); F. Chiappa, *Il papiro Busca* (Milan, 1972); U. Luft, *ZÄS* 104 (1977): 46–75 and M. H. van Es, *ZÄS* 109 (1982): 97–121 (Ptahmose); E. Dondelinger, *Papyrus Ani* (Graz, 1978); E. von Dassow, ed., with a translation by R. O. Faulkner and O. Goelet, *The Egyptian Book of the Dead: The Book of Going Forth by Day* (San Francisco, 1994; Ani). A list of sixty–seven textual sources from the Ramesside Period is given by I. Munro, *Untersuchungen* (see above, under Dynasty 18), pp. 296–308.

Third Intermediate Period: A systematic survey is found in A. Niwiński, *Studies on the Illustrated Theban Funerary Papyri of the 11th and 10th Centuries B.C.,* OBO 86 (Freiburg and Göttingen, 1989); individual manuscripts, P. Guieysse and E. Lefébure, *Le papyrus funéraire de Soutimès* (Paris, 1877); E. A. W. Budge, *The Greenfield Papyrus* (London, 1912); E. Naville, *Papyrus funéraires de la XXIe dynastie,* 2 vols. (Paris, 1912 and 1914); M. Heerma van Voss, *Zwischen Grab und Paradies* (Basel, 1971; Tajuherit, Leiden T 3); M. Valloggia, in *Mélanges Jacques Jean Clère,* CRIPEL 13 (Lille, 1991), pp. 129–136 (P. Bodmer); I. Munro, *Der Totenbuch-Papyrus des Hohenpriesters Pa-nedjem II. (pLondon BM 10793/pCampbell)* (Wiesbaden, 1996).

Late Period: F. M. H. Haekal, *ASAE* 63 (1979): 51–78 (Ankhefenkhons, Cairo): U. Verhoeven, *Das saitische Totenbuch der Iahtesnacht: P. Colon. Aeg. 10207,* PTA 41 (Bonn, 1993; includes references to other Saite Period manuscripts); F. Tiradritti and G. Rosati, in *Vicino Oriente IX—1993* (Rome, 1994; tomb of Shoshenq, TT 27). Adding to the edition of Lepsius, further spells were published by W. Pleyte, *Chapitres supplémentaires du Livre des Morts* (Leiden, 1881) and provided with the numbers 166–174 (not identical to the corresponding numbers in the editions of Naville and Budge).

Ptolemaic and Roman Periods: F. Lexa, *Das demotische Totenbuch der Pariser Nationalbibliothek* (Leipzig, 1910); T. Andrzejewski, *Rocznik Orientalistyczny* 20 (1956): 83–109 (Pasherenmin, in Cracow and Louvre; cf. M. Barwik, *RdE* 46 (1995): 3–7); B. de Rachewiltz, *Il Libro dei Morti degli antichi Egiziani* (Milan, 1958; Iufankh, in Turin); J. C. Guillevic and P. Ramond, *L. Papyrus Varille* (Toulouse, 1975); L. Limme, in H. de Meulenaere and L. Limme, eds., *Artibus Aegypti: Studia in honorem Bernardi V. Bothmer* (Brussels, 1983), pp. 81–96 (three papyri in Brussels); J. J. Clère, *Le papyrus de Nesmin: Un Livre des Morts hiéroglyphique de l'époque ptolémaïque,* BG 10 (Cairo, 1987); Ch. Sturtewagen, *The Funerary Papyrus Palau Rib. Nr. Inv. 450* (Barcelona, 1991; improvements by Ch. Karcher and Ch. C. Van Siclen III, *VA* 7 (1991): 169–176); A. de Caluwe, *Un Livre des Morts sur bandelette de momie* (Brussels, 1991; Brussels E.6179).

Recent text editions of individual spells from papyri of the New Kingdom: B. Lüscher, *Totenbuch Spruch 1 nach Quellen des Neuen Reiches* (Wiesbaden, 1986); G. P. Laan, *Niet ten dode opgeschreven* (diss. Amsterdam University, 1995; spell 71); see also the treatments of individual spells cited below.

Further studies

Third Intermediate Period: M. Heerma van Voss, in U. Verhoeven and E. Graefe, eds., *Religion und Philosophie im alten Ägypten: Festgabe für Philippe Derchain zu seinem 65. Geburtsdag am 24. Juli 1991*, OLA 39 (Louvain, 1991), pp. 155–157 (Pinudjem I); L. H. Lesko, in D. P. Silverman, ed., *For His Ka: Essays Offered in Memory of Klaus Baer*, SAOC 55 (Chicago, 1994), pp. 179–186 (Pinudjem I and Pinudjem II).

Late Period: M. Mosher, *The Ancient Egyptian Book of the Dead in the Late Period* (diss. University of California at Berkeley, 1990; cf. idem, *JARCE* 29 (1992): 143–172.

G. Maspero's survey of the content in *RHR* 15 (1887): 266–316 was reprinted in his *Études de mythologie et d'archéologie égyptiennes*, vol. 1 (Paris, 1893), pp. 325–387. After the earliest translations by Birch and Pierret, P. Le Page Renouf published an English translation relying on Naville's edition in *PSBA* 14–19 (1892–1897) up to spell 139, which was continued by E. Naville, ibid. 24–26 (1902–1904), with additional vignettes. This translation appeared as a separate volume under the title *The Egyptian Book of the Dead* (London, 1904), but it never enjoyed the circulation attained by the English translation of E. A. W. Budge, which first appeared in 1901 under the title *The Chapters of Coming Forth by Day*, of which there have been innumerable reprints. More recent comprehensive translations have been made by P. Barguet, *Le Livre des Morts des anciens Égyptiens* (Paris, 1967), with a rich bibliography; T. G. Allen, ed. E. B. Hauser, *The Book of the Dead or Going Forth by Day: Ideas of the Ancient Egyptians Concerning the Hereafter as Expressed in Their Own Terms*, SAOC 37 (Chicago, 1974); E. Hornung, *Das Totenbuch der Ägypter* (Zurich, 1979; rpt. 1993), and R. O. Faulkner, ed. C. Andrews, *The Ancient Egyptian Book of the Dead* (London, 1985). See also U. Verhoeven, *Das saitische Totenbuch der Iahtesnacht* (Bonn, 1993), vol. 1, pp. 73 ff., on the general problem of translation. A rich selection is given by S. Donadoni, *Testi religiosi egizi* (Turin, 1970), pp. 255–328. On the problem of dating, see M. Heerma van Voss, *Phoenix* 23 (1977): 84–89.

Detailed treatments of individual spells: W. Czermak, *ZÄS* 76 (1940); 9–24 (spell 1); H. D. Schneider, *Shabtis*, vol. 1 (Leiden 1977), pp. 78–80. (spell 6); W. Westendorf, ed., *Göttinger Totenbuchstudien: Beiträge zum 17. Kapitel*, GO 3 (Wiesbaden, 1975; spell 17); on the textual history of spell 17, U. Rössler-Köhler, *Kapitel 17 des ägyptischen Totenbuches: Untersuchungen zur Textgeschichte und Funktion eines Textes der altägyptischen Totenliteratur*, GO 10 (Wiesbaden, 1979), and on the textual history also eadem, in U. Verhoeven and E. Graefe, eds., *Religion und Philosophie im alten Ägypten*, FS Ph. Derchain (Leuven, 1991), pp. 277–291; H. Kees, *Göttinger Totenbuchstudien: Totenbuch Kapitel 69 und 70*, UGAAe (Berlin, 1954; chapters 69 and 70); G. P. Laan, *Niet ten dode opgeschreven* (diss. Amsterdam University, 1995; spell 71); P. Vernus, *Athribis* (Cairo, 1978), pp. 270–277 (spell 88); H. Kees, in *Miscellanea Berolinensia*, vol. 2/2 (Berlin, 1950), pp. 77–96 (spell 99A); Ch. Kuentz, *BIFAO* 30 (1931): 823–880 (spell 106); K. Sethe et al., *Die Sprüche für das Kennen der Seelen der heiligen Orte* (Leipzig, 1925), which is a collection of articles from *ZÄS* 57 (1922)–59 (1924) dealing with spells 108–109 and 112–116); Ch. Maystre, *Les Déclarations d'innocence* (Cairo, 1937; spell 125); U. Verhoeven, *RdE* 43 (1992): 169–194 (spell 146, end; see also F. Tiradritti, *Vicino Oriente IX—1993* (Rome, 1994), pp. 71–106); R. El-Sayed, *MDAIK* 36 (1980): 357–390 (spell 148); B. Lüscher, *Untersuchungen zu Totenbuch Spruch 151* (diss. Basel University, as yet unpublished; spell 151); D. Bidoli, *Die Sprüche der Fangnetze in den altägyptischen Sargtexten*, ADAIK 9 (Glückstadt, 1976; spell 153); J. Yoyotte, *RdE* 29 (1977): 194–200 (spells 162–167); M. Mosher, *JARCE* 29 (1992) 158–169 (spell 163); J. Černý, *BIFAO* 41 (1942): 118–133 (Pleyte 166); G. Burkard, *Spätzeitliche Osiris-Liturgien im Corpus der Asasif-Papyri* (Wiesbaden, 1995), pp. 23–62 (Pleyte 168 and 169); H. Kees, *ZÄS* 65 (1930): 65–83 (spell 175); C. de Wit, *BiOr* 10 (1953): 90–94 (spell 181); T. G. Allen, *JNES* 11 (1952): 177–186 (spells 191–192, though according to J.-C. Goyon, *Studia Aegyptiaca*, Budapest, 1974, vol. 1, pp. 117–127, these belong to an entirely different composition); M. Heerma van Voss *De spreuk om de kisten te kennen* (Leiden, 1971; spell 193); T. DuQuesne, *At the Court of Osiris: Book of the Dead Spell 194, a Rare Egyptian Judgment Text*, OCE 4 (London, 1994).

On vignettes: Ch. Beinlich-Seeber, *Untersuchungen zur Darstellung des Totengerichts im Alten Ägypten*, MÄS 35 (Berlin, 1976); H. Milde, *The Vignettes in the Book of the Dead of Neferrenpet* (Leiden, 1991); P. Eschweiler, *Bildzauber im alten Ägypten*, OBO 137 (Freiburg and Göttingen, 1994), pp. 161 ff.

On the meaning of the spells, see further: R. El-Sayed, *BSEG* 9/10 (1984/85): 245–274 (the role of light). More comprehensive studies of the content of the Book of the Dead have yet to be made. On its use by Ezra Pound (after the edition of Budge), see G. Schmidt, *Arcadia* 6 (1971): 297–301.

An esoteric literature is also connected with the Book of the Dead in which names such as S. Mayassis, A. Champdor, and G. Kolpaktchy are prominent; their free renderings have found a wide circulation in other disciplines. The interpretation of the Book of the Dead as an initiatory text began already with the theosophist H. P. Blavatsky, *Isis Unveiled: A Master Key to the Mysteries of Ancient and Modern Science and Theology* (New York, 1877), who relied on the first English translation by S. Birch, and it has continued down to Mayassis.

The Books of Breathing

For the manuscript published by V. Denon, see the atlas of his *Voyage dans la Basse et la Haute-Égypte pendant les campagnes du général Bonaparte* (Paris, 1804), plate 136; this volume was translated into English by Arthur Aiken under the title *Travels in Upper and Lower Egypt during the Campaigns of General Bonaparte in that Country* (New York, 1803). This version was treated by H. Brugsch, *S'ai en sinsin* (Berlin, 1851).

As yet, no edition of all the texts is available. The best summary is that given by J.-C. Goyon, *Rituels funéraires de l'ancienne Égypte* (Paris, 1972), with translation. There are lists of manuscripts in Goyon, ibid., pp. 349–350 and M. Bellion, *Catalogue des manuscrits* (1987; see above under Book of the Dead). There have since been publications of further manuscripts: M. Coenen and J. Quaegebeur, *De Papyrus Denon in het Museum Meermanno-Westreenianum, Den Haag, of Het Boek van het*

Ademen van Isis (Leuven, 1995; manuscript in The Hague); Liebieghaus, Museum Alter Plastik, *Ägyptische Bildwerke*, vol. 3 (Melsungen, 1993), no. 63 (manuscript in Frankfurt); M. Valloggia, in *Hommages à la mémoire de Serge Sauneron, 1927–1976*, vol. 1, BE 81 (Cairo, 1979), pp. 285–304 (manuscript in Lausanne); W. Brunch in *Studien zu Sprache und Religion Ägyptens zu Ehren von Wolfhart Westendorf* (Göttingen, 1984), pp. 455–460 (Demotic manuscript in Munich); and A. Gasse, *Les papyrus hiératiques et hiéroglyphiques du Museo Gregoriano Egizio* (Vatican City, 1993). Of the older editions, we can cite here P. J. Horrack, *Le Livre des Respirations d'après les manuscrits du Musée du Louvre* (Paris, 1877) and Jens D. C. Lieblein, *Le livre égyptien . . . "que mon nom fleurisse"* (Leipzig, 1895). Both books were also printed in hieroglyphic type in E. A. W. Budge, *The Chapters of Coming Forth by Day or The Theban Recension of the Book of the Dead*, vol. 3 (London, 1910), pp. 133–150. A Demotic text combining the Opening of the Mouth Ritual and the Books of Breathing has been published by M. Smith, *The Liturgy of the Opening of the Mouth for Breathing* (Oxford, 1993).

On the meaning of the content and on the connection with divine decrees and Hermetic writings, see also J. Quaegebeur, in T. DuQuesne (ed.), *Hermes Aegyptiacus: Egyptological Studies for B. H. Stricker* (Oxford, 1995), pp. 157–181.

The New Kingdom Books of the Netherworld

General

Most of the Books of the Netherworld are translated and provided with an introduction in E. Hornung, *Ägyptische Unterweltsbücher*, 3d ed. (Zurich, 1989), with an index by L. Spycher; there is an unrevised reprint with the title *Die Unterweltsbücher der Ägypter* (Zurich, 1992).

For general surveys of the genre, see A. Piankoff, *ASAE* 40 (1940): 283–289; H. Altenmüller, in *Handbuch der Orientalistik*, vol. 1 (Ägyptologie), sec. 2 (Literatur), 2d ed. (Leiden, 1970), pp. 69–81; W. Barta, *Die Bedeutung der Jenseitsbücher für den verstorbenen König*, MÄS 42 (Munich, 1985); idem, *Komparative Untersuchungen zu vier Unterweltsbüchern: Das altägyptische Zweiwegebuch und seine Topographie*, MÄU 1 (Frankfurt a. M., 1990); E. Hermsen, *Die zwei Wege des Jenseits: Das altägyptische Zweiwegebuch und seine Topographie*, OBO 112 (Freiburgand Göttingen, 1991), pp. 32–47. On the concluding scenes that summarize the course of the sun, see E. Hornung, *MDAIK* 37 (1981): 217–226, and on the entire genre see also H. Brunner, *SAK* 8 (1980): 79–84 (with emphasis on the inclusion of the course of the sun in the royal tombs) and idem, in G. Stephenson, ed., *Leben und Tod in den Religionen: Symbol und Wirklichkeit* (Darmstadt, 1980), pp. 215–228. On the use of the books in the tomb of Sethos I, see E. Hornung, *Eranos Jahrbuch* 50 (1981): 431–475. On the scenes of the course of the sun, see idem, *Eranos Jahrbuch* 48 (1979): 183–237 and idem, in *Sesto Congresso internaz. di Egittologia, Atti*, vol. 1 (Turin, 1992), pp. 317–323.

The Egyptian title of the genre is discussed by A. Piankoff, *BIFAO* 62 (1964): 147–149. In the same volume, pp. 207–218, he mentions possible connections with the religion of Akhenaten; in this connection, see also E. Hornung, *BSEG* 13 (1989): 65–68, indicating fundamental differences. F. Abitz, *Pharao als Gott in den Unterweltsbüchern des Neuen Reiches*, OBO 146 (Freiburg and Göttingen, 1995), treats the concrete references to the king and additional insertions in the individual books.

On the explanation of the books as instructions proposed by S. Morenz, see E. Hornung, in E. Hornung and O. Keel, eds., *Studien zur altägyptischen Lebenslehren*, OBO 28 (Freiburg and Göttingen, 1979), pp. 217–224, where differences from the instruction genre are emphasized. Anthropological questions concerning the Books of the Netherworld are treated by A. Rupp, *Vergehen und Bleiben: Religionsgeschichtliche Studien zum Personenverständnis in Ägypten und im Alten Testament* (Saarbrücken, 1976); see also idem, *ZÄS* 101 (1974): 35–49.

U. Rossler-Köhler, ASAE 70 (1985): 383–408, offers a fundamental study of the unusual omissions of text, leaving empty spaces, that appear in many versions of the Books of the Netherworld and succeeds in suggesting rather varied reasons for them: in part, they simply serve the arrangement; additionally, they can indicate symbolic spaces in which the indication of enemies is not written out. The many punishment scenes in the Place of Annihilation are comprehensively treated by E. Hornung, *Altägyptische Höllenvorstellungen*, ASAW 59/3 (Berlin, 1968) and idem, in T. Schabert and E. Hornung, eds., *Strukturen des Chaos*, Eranos NS 2 (Munich, 1994), pp. 227–262; there is an English version of the latter in *Diogenes* 165 (1994): 133–156, and a French version in *Diogène* 165 (1994): 121–143.

The Amduat

Maspero's first detailed survey and partial translation in *RHR* 17 (1888): 251–310 was reprinted in G. Maspero, *Les hypogées royaux de Thèbes*, EMAE 2 (Paris, 1893), pp. 1–181; Maspero employed the verion of Sethos I, along with certain papyri for the last hour. His pupil G. Jéquier published the first edition of the short version: *Le Livre de ce qu'il y a dans l'Hadès: Version abrégée* (Paris, 1894), mainly from versions on papyri of Dynasty 21; R. V. Lanzone had already published a papyrus in Turin, *Le domicile des esprits* (Paris, 1879). A description and translation of both versions, with the text in hieroglyphic type following Lefébure's copy of Sethos I and Lanzone for the twelfth hour, was published by E. A. W. Budge, *The Egyptian Heaven and Hell*, 3 vols. (London, 1905; rpt., 1 vol., 1925); the long version fills vol. 1 while the short version (from the tomb of Sethos I and Leiden T. 71) is dealt with in vol. 2, pp. 1–40. He had already supplied descriptions of the hours in *The Gods of the Egyptians*, vol. 1 (London, 1904). Paul Bucher published the concluding texts of the first three hours in *BIFAO* 30 (1931): 229–247. The text volume (pt. 1) of E. Hornung, *Das Amduat; Die Schrift des Verborgenen Raumes*, ÄgAbh 7 (Wiesbaden, 1963) has now been replaced by idem, *Texte zum Amduat*, 3 vols. with continuous pagination, AH 13–15 (Geneva, 1987–1994) and hand copies by L. Spycher and B. Lüscher; both editions take into account only the versions from the New Kingdom, down to Ramesses IX. A revision of the commentary (pt. 2, 1963) is planned; pt. 3 (ÄgAbh 13, 1967) contains the short version, whose text appears again in a synoptic edition in *Texte zum Amduat*, pp. 1–97. There is also a German translation in E. Hornung, *Ägyptische Unterweltsbücher*, 3d ed. (Zurich, 1989), pp. 57–194, and an English translation in A. Piankoff, *The Tomb of Ramesses VI*, Bollingen Series 40/1 (New York, 1954), pp. 227–318; the introductions to the individual hours have also been translated in M. Clagett, *Ancient Egyptian Science: A Source Book*, vol. 1 (Philadelphia,

1989), pp. 491–506. Additional text fragments are expected from the work of E. Brock on the royal sarcophagi of the Ramesside Period.

There is a survey of the New Kingdom versions in Hornung, *Texte zum Amduat,* vol. 1, pp. x–xvi. The version from the tomb of Tuthmosis III is now published by A. Fornari and M. Tosi, *Nella sede della verità: Deir el Medina e l'ipogeo di Thutmosi III* (Milan, 1987), with color reproductions, though without the short version or the catalogue of deities, for which there exist excellent, unpublished black-and-white photographs by H. Burton. Samples of the fragments from the tomb of Tuthmosis I are reproduced in G. Daressy, *Fouilles de la Vallée des Rois* (Cairo, 1902), plate LVII and K. Myśliwiec, *Studien zum Gott Atum,* vol. 1, HÄB 5 (Hildesheim, 1978), plates XIX–XX. The preliminary report on the version of Useramun by E. Hornung, *Die Grabkammer des Vezirs User,* NAWG 1961/5 has now been replaced by the contribution in E. Dziobek, *Die Gräber des Vezirs User-Amun: Theben Nr. 61 und 131* (Mainz, 1994), pp. 42–47. Individual hours from the tomb of Amenophis II are reproduced in Hornung, *Valley of the Kings: Horizon of Eternity,* trans. David Warburton (New York, 1990), pp. 81 (second hour), 102 (twelfth hour), 111 (seventh hour), and 144 (tenth hour) and in A. Champdor, *Livre des Morts,* pp. 116–117 (fourth hour); his entire tomb has been published only by P. Bucher, *Les textes des tombes de Thoutmosis III et d'Aménophis II,* MIFAO 60 (Cairo, 1932). There are color details from the version on the shrine of Tutankhamun in Kamal el-Mallakh and A. C. Brackman, *The Gold of Tutankhamen* (New York, 1978), plates 20–24; facsimiles of both hours are given by A. Piankoff, *Les chapelles de Tout-Ankh-Amon,* MIFAO 72 (Cairo, 1952), plates VI and VIII, and see idem, *The Shrines of Tut-Ankh-Amun,* Bollingen Series 40/2 (New York, 1955), plates 30–36.

For Sethos I, see H. Burton and E. Hornung, *The Tomb of Pharaoh Seti I / Das Grab Sethos' I.* (Zurich, 1991). For two extracts from the tomb of Ramesses IV, see E. Hornung, *Zwei ramessidische Königsgräber: Ramses IV. und Ramses VII.,* Theben 11 (Mainz, 1990), pp. 84–85. For Ramesses VI, see A. Piankoff, *The Tomb of Ramesses VI,* Bollingen Series 40/1 (New York, 1954), plates 74–101, and on the order of the hours in this tomb, see F. Abitz, *Baugeschichte und Dekoration des Grabes Ramses' VI.,* OBO 89 (Freiburg and Göttingen, 1989), pp. 99–110. For Ramesses IX, see F. Guilmant, *Le tombeau de Ramsès IX,* MIFAO 15 (Cairo, 1907), plates 38, 43–44, 63, 65–75, and 92, supplemented by F. Abitz, *SAK* 17 (1990): 1–40. As a result of the most recent restoration work in the antechamber to the sarcophagus chamber in the tomb of Siptah, traces of the sixth hour are now visible, though they are without texts.

The Dynasty 21 papyri in the Cairo Museum have been published by A. F. Sadek, *Contribution à l'étude de l'Amdouat,* OBO 65 (Freiburg and Göttingen, 1985), with a translation of the ninth through the twelfth hour, and the fragments from the cenotaph of Iuput (portions of the first, tenth, and twelfth hours) have been published by P. Vernus, *BIFAO* 75 (1975): 67–72. For further papyri, see E. Hornung, *Das Amduat,* Part III (Berlin 3001); L. H. Lesko, in *Studies in Honor of George R. Hughes: January 12, 1977,* SAOC 39 (Chicago, 1976), pp. 133–138; A. Abdelhamid Youssef, *BIFAO* 82 (1982): 1–17 (Cairo J. 96638, short version); M. Heerma van Voss, in M. Heerma van Voss, ed., *Studies in Egyptian Religion Dedicated to Professor Jan Zandee* (Leiden, 1982), pp. 56–60 (Houston); M. Valloggia, *RdE* 40 (1989): 131–144 (P. Bodmer 107, combined with a solar hymn); A. F. Sadek, *VA* 7 (1991): 5–14 (Marseille, with figures from the third hour); M. Heerma van Voss, in *L'Egitto fuori dell'Egitto* (Bologna, 1991), pp. 451–453 (Kansas City 33–1398, figures from the eleventh hour); S. Quirke, *JEA* 80 (1994): 147–149 (Wellcome Institute, with figures from the first, third, eleventh, and twelfth hours); M. Heerma van Voss, *JEOL* 33 (1995): 21–30 (papyrus in Antwerp, mixed with motifs from the Book of the Dead). A detailed listing and classification of the papyri has been published by A. Niwiński, *Studies on the Illustrated Theban Funerary Papyri of the 11th and 10th Centuries B.C.*, OBO 86 (Freiburg and Göttingen, 1989).

Most of the Late Period versions in tombs and on sarcophagi remain unpublished. For Petamenophis (TT 33), see F. W. von Bissing, *ZÄS* 74 (1938): 21–22 and A. Piankoff, "Le Livre de l'Am-Duat et les variantes tardives," in O. Firchow, ed., *Ägyptologische Studien*, DAWBIO 29 (Berlin, 1955), pp. 244–247 (with a photograph of the fifth hour); excerpts from the twelfth hour in the tomb of Mutirdis (TT 410) are published by J. Assmann, *Das Grab der Mutirdis* (Mainz, 1977), pp. 75–77. For the sarcophagi, see H. Jenni, *Das Dekorationsprogramm des Sarkophages Nektanebos' II.*, AH 12 (Geneva, 1986). Two scenes with captions on the walls of a burial chamber of Dynasty 26 date are published by E. el-Sawi and F. Gomaà, *Das Grab des Panehsi, Gottesvaters von Heliopolis in Matariya*, ÄAT 23 (Wiesbaden, 1993). Some hours (the seventh, tenth, and eleventh) are attested on blocks from the nilometer at Roda; there are photographs in the Dossier Drioton in the Strasbourg library. A remark regarding the copy of the book (with its exact title) on the sarcophagus of Tjaihorpata from the reign of Nectanebo II is treated by J. Baines, *JEA* 78 (1992): 247. The citations on coffins of the early Ptolemaic Period are found in O. Neugebauer and R. A. Parker, *Egyptian Astronomical Texts*, vol. 3, BES 6 (Providence and London, 1969), p. 61 with plate 28, and J. Assmann, *MDAIK* 23 (1968): 22 with fig. 2.

The edition by G. Maspero first appeared in *RHR* 17 (1888): 251–310 and was reprinted in his *Études de mythologie et d'archéologie égyptienne*, vol. 2 (Paris, 1893), pp. 1–181 (esp. pp. 27–163); it was the basis for the surveys of the content of the book in A. Wiedemann, *Die Religion der alten Ägypter* (Münster i.W., 1890), pp. 47–55 and E. Naville, *La religion des anciens Égyptiens* (Paris, 1906), pp. 77–87. E. A. W. Budge gave a more detailed treatment of the individual hours in *The Gods of the Egyptians* (London, 1904), vol. 1, pp. 204–260, and see also above in idem, *The Egyptian Heaven and Hell* (1905). B. de Rachewiltz, *Il libro egizio degli inferi*, 2d ed. (Rome, 1982) for the most part translates only the introductions to the hours, while further passages are given by S. Donadoni, *Testi religiosi egizi* (Turin, 1970), pp. 329–333. The survey by H. Kees in H. Bonnet, *Reallexikon der ägyptische Religionsgeschichte* (Berlin, 1952), pp. 17–20, reflects the negative evaluation of the book by A. Erman.

On questions of form and content, S. Schott, *Die Schrift der verborgenen Kammer in Königsgräbern der 18. Dynastie*, NAWG 1958/4 and H. Altenmüller, *JEOL* 20 (1968): 27–42 (on the problem of the "gaps"), are still important. The formulae regarding knowledge are treated by E. F. Wente, *JNES* 41 (1982): 162–167. A more recent survey of the contents is given by K. Koch, *Geschichte der ägyptischen Religion* (Stuttgart, 1993), pp. 304–313, and S. Binder, *BACE* 6 (1995): 7–30. On the meaning of the fifth hour of the night, see S. Schott, *Zum Weltbild der Jenseitsführer des neuen Reiches*, NAWG 1965/11, pp. 191–193.

In more recent times, a dating of the composition earlier than the New Kingdom, for the most part to the Middle Kingdom, has been favored by, among others, S. Morenz, *Eranos Jahrbuch* 34 (1965): 436, n. 28, and (with less certainty) idem, *TL* 90 (1965): 503; H. Altenmüller, *JEOL* 20 (1968) 42, and idem, *Handbuch der Orientalistik*, vol. 1 (Ägyptologie), sec. 1, pt. 2 (Leiden, 1970), p. 72 (dating it to perhaps as early as the Old Kingdom); E. F. Wente, *JNES* 41 (1982): 175–176, and idem, *JNES* 42 (1983): 156; and J. Baines, *JEA* 76 (1990): 63.

A first attempt to see the Amduat not only as a cosmography but also as an internal journey was undertaken by B. George, *GM* 3 (1972): 15–20, and there is now a fundamentally important elaboration by A. Schweizer, *Seelenführer durch den verborgenen Raum: Das ägyptische Unterweltsbuch Amduat* (Munich, 1994), while E. Hornung has highlighted the most important stages in the journey through the netherworld in the Amduat and the Book of Gates in *Die Nachtfahrt der Sonne: Eine altägyptische Beschreibung des Jenseits* (Zurich, 1991). A psychological interpretation of the Amduat has also been attempted by G. Schoeller, *Isis: Auf der Suche nach dem göttlichen Geheimnis* (Munich, 1991), pp. 131–214. On the relationship between picture and text, see N. Hoffmann, *ZÄS* 123 (1996): 26–40. The order of the hours is treated by W. Barta, *JEOL* 21 (1970): 164–168 (tomb of Tuthmosis III), and idem, *BO* 31 (1974): 197–201 (Ramesside tombs). The explanation of the Amduat as a royal burial ritual offered by P. Barguet, *RdE* 24 (1972): 7–11, is unconvincing; see the detailed remarks by W. Barta, *Die Bedeutung der Jenseitsbücher*, MÄS 42 (Munich, 1985), pp. 154–159. Ch. Leitz, *Studien zur ägyptischen Astronomie*, 2d ed., ÄgAbh 49 (Wiesbaden, 1991), pp. 101–104, sees in the statements regarding distances in the first hour an indication that the Egyptians of that era had already recognized that the world is a sphere and had determined its circumference more exactly than Eratosthenes; see the critical remarks by K. Ferrari d'Occhieppo, R. Krauss, and Th. Schmidt-Kaler, *ZÄS* 123 (1996): 103–110.

The continuation of motifs from the Amduat down into Islamic times has been treated by I. Grumach, *ASP* 7 (1970): 169–181.

The Spell of the Twelve Caverns

There was an early publication of the fragmentary version in the Osireion by M. A. Murray, *The Osireion at Abydos* (London, 1904), plates II–V; most of the remaining sources, with translation and commentary, are published in A. Piankoff, *The Wandering of the Soul*, Bollingen Series 40/6 (Princeton, 1974), pp. 40–114 and plates 10–42. A partial translation into German is found in E. Hornung, *Das Totenbuch der Ägypter* (Zurich, 1979), pp. 341–343, and a more detailed description and translation in Th. G. Allen, *The Book of the Dead or Going Forth by Day* (Chicago, 1974), pp. 162–175.

The Book of Gates

J. Bonomi and S. Sharpe, *The Alabaster Sarcophagus of Oimeneptah I., King of Egypt* (London, 1864), is the first, and today still the authoritative, facsimile edition of the version on the alabaster sarcophagus of Sethos I in Sir John Soane's Museum in

London; it served as the basis for subsequent studies by E. Lefébure, *Records of the Past*, vol. 10 (London, 1878), pp. 79–134, and vol. 12 (London, 1881), pp. 1–35; G. Maspero, *RHR* 18 (1888); and E. A. W. Budge, *The Egyptian Heaven and Hell* (London, 1905). The first synoptic text edition, in hieroglyphic type, of all the versions of the New Kingdom by Ch. Maystre and A. Piankoff, *Le Livre des Portes*, 3 vols, MIFAO 74, 75, and 90 (Cairo 1939–1962), with portions also in *ASAE* 55 (1958) and 56 (1959) is now replaced by E. Hornung, *Das Buch von den Pforten des Jenseits*, 2 vols., AH 7 and 8 (Geneva, 1979–1984), with an autographed text by A. Brodbeck in the first volume and a translation and commentary in the second volume. The fragments of the alabaster coffin of Siptah in the Metropolitan Museum of Art in New York that was inscribed on both the outside and the inside, like that of Sethos, remain unstudied.

There are photographic reproductions of the version of Haremhab in E. Hornung (with F. Teichmann), *Das Grab des Haremhab im Tal der Könige* (Bern, 1971); of that of Ramesses I in A. Piankoff, *La tombe de Ramsès Ier*, BIFAO 56 (1957), pp. 189–200 with plates IV–VII; of that of Sethos I in H. Burton and E. Hornung, *The Tomb of Pharaoh Seti I / Das Grab Sethos' I*. (Zurich, 1991); of that of Ramesses IV and Ramesses VII in E. Hornung, *Zwei ramessidische Königsgräber: Ramses IV. und Ramses VII.* (Mainz, 1990), plates 60–67 and 101–103; of that of Ramesses VI in Piankoff, *The Tomb of Ramesses VI*, Bollingen Series 40/1 (New York, 1954), plates 37–62. For Tjanefer, see the line drawings in K. C. Seele, *The Tomb of Tjanefer at Thebes* (Chicago, 1959), plates 30–38.

The concluding representation from the papyrus of Anhai was first reproduced in E. A. W. Budge, *Facsimiles of the Papyri of Hunefer, Anhai, Kerasher and Netchemet* (London, 1899), plate 8, and since, in other publications as well. On the Papyrus of Khonsumes, see A. Piankoff and N. Rambova, *Mythological Papyri*, Bollingen Series 40/3 (New York, 1957), no. 30, and on Mutirdis, see J. Assmann, *Das Grab der Mutirdis* (Mainz, 1977), p. 75 (with the concluding representation and the third gate). G. Maspero dealt briefly with the contents in *Études de mythologie et d'archéologie égyptiens*, vol. 2 (Paris, 1893), pp. 163–181, making reference to the English translation by E. Lefébure in *Records of the Past*, vols. 10 and 12 (see above). H. Brugsch discusses the concluding representation in detail in *Religion und Mythologie der alten Aegypter*, 2d ed. (Leipzig, 1891), pp. 216–221, while A. Wiedemann offers a short survey in *Die Religion der alten Ägypter* (Münster i.W., 1890), pp. 55–58. E. A. W. Budge, *The Egyptian Heaven and Hell*, 3 vols. (London, 1905; reprint ed., 1925), gives a translation and description of the version on the sarcophagus of Sethos I in vol. 2, and in vol. 3, pp. 103–199, a comparison of the hours of the night with those in the Amduat, with a false count after the fifth hour, because he arranged the fragments of the lid incorrectly. A brief survey is also offered by H. Bonnet, *Reallexikon der ägyptischen Religionsgeschichte* (Berlin, 1952), pp. 589–590. More recent English translations are given in Piankoff, *The Tomb of Ramesses VI*, Bollingen Series 40/1 (New York, 1954), pp. 137–224, and J. Zandee, in *Liber Amicorum: Studies in Honour of C. J. Bleeker* (Leiden, 1969), pp. 282–324 (utilizing Piankoff's division of the hours). There is a first translation into German by Hornung, *Die Unterweltsbücher der Ägypter* (Zurich, 1992), pp. 195–308.

On the hall of judgment (scene 33), see M. Heerma van Voss, in *Travels in the World of the Old Testament: Studies Presented to M. A. Beek* (Assen, 1974), pp. 80–90.

The "posts of Geb" in scene 45 are discussed by F. T. Miosi, *JSSEA* 12 (1982): 77–80. On the griffin in scene 61, see W. Barta, *JEOL* 23 (1975): 343–344. On scene 76, see M. Clagett, *Ancient Egyptian Science: A Source Book*, vol. 1 (Philadelphia, 1989), p. 482. On the conlcuding representation, see A. Niwiński, *GM* 65 (1983): 79–85. On the remarks regarding offerings, see E. F. Wente, *JNES* 41 (1982): 168–175. Against the interpretation of the book as a ritual for transferring rule from the deceased king to his successor, offered by P. Barguet, *RdE* 27 (1975): 30–36, see W. Barta, *Die Bedeutung der Jenseitsbücher für den verstorbenen König*, MÄS 42 (1985), pp. 159–162.

The Enigmatic Book of the Netherworld

The two sections are published in facsimile by A. Piankoff, *Les Chapelles de Tout-Ankh-Amon*, MIFAO 72 (Cairo, 1952), plates II (section B) and IV (section A), and with photographs as well in idem, *The Shrines of Tut-Ankh-Amon*, Bollingen Series 40/2 (New York, 1955), plates 47–53 and in K. el-Mallakh and A. C. Brackman, *The Gold of Tutankhamen* (New York, 1978), plates 29–36. On the enigmatic writing of the texts in sec. A, see E. Drioton, *JEA* 35 (1949): 117–122, and also A. Piankoff, ibid., pp. 113–116, on the figure of the large god. On the concluding representation, see K. Myśliwiec, *Bulletin du Centenaire*, supplement to *BIFAO* 83 (Cairo, 1981), p. 94. There are descriptions and translations of both sections by E. Hornung, *JSSEA* 13 (1983): 29–34, and a summary by W. Barta, which includes the Book of the Dead spells, in his *Die Bedeutung der Jenseitsbücher*, MÄS 42 (1985), pp. 67–68 and 128–130. New, improved readings and interpretations have now been supplied by J. C. Darnell in his as yet unpublished dissertation, "The Enigmatic Netherworld Books of the Solar-Osirian Unity: Cryptographic Compositions in the Tombs of Tutankhamun, Ramesses VI, and Ramesses IX" (University of Chicago, 1995).

The Book of Caverns

The only publication of the composition, with the text and a translation into French, is by A. Piankoff, *Le Livre de Quérerts* (Cairo, 1946); this is a collection of articles that had appeared in *BIFAO* 41 (1943), 42 (1944), 43 (1945), and 45 (1947). An English translation is supplied by Piankoff in *The Tomb of Ramesses VI*, Bollingen Series 40/1 (New York, 1954), and a German translation by E. Hornung, *Die Unterweltsbücher der Ägypter*, (Zurich, 1992), pp. 311–424. There is a translation of the first section by S. Donadoni, *Testi religiosi egizi* (Turin, 1970), pp. 336–341. A summary is provided in D. Meeks and Chr. Favard–Meeks, *La vie quotidienne des dieux égyptiens* (Paris, 1993), pp. 221–239, translated into English by G. M. Goshgarian under the title *Daily Life of the Egyptian Gods* (Ithaca, 1997), pp. 151–162, and in W. Barta, *Die Bedeutung der Jenseitstexte für den verstorbenen König*, MÄS 42 (Munich, 1985) pp. 60–65 and 110–123. G. Roulin is presently preparing a new edition of the book.

The version in the Osireion was published by H. Frankfort, *The Cenotaph of Seti I at Abydos* (London, 1933), vol. 2, plates 23–49; the first English translation appears in ibid., vol. 1, pp. 36–65. There are color photographs of the figures of Nut and Osiris from section five of the version in the tomb of Ramesses VI in E. Hornung, *Tal der Könige: Die Ruhestätte der Pharaonen* (Mainz, 1990), p. 131, fig. 101 and p. 159, fig. 129; the concluding representation is reproduced in ibid., p. 118, fig. 93, and for the variants of the concluding representation from the tombs of Merneptah and Twosre, see ibid., p. 65, fig. 45–46. For Ramesses IV and Ramesses VII, see E. Hornung, *Zwei ramessidische Königsgräber: Ramses IV. und Ramses VII.* (Mainz, 1990), pp. 86–87 and plates 44–50, 76–83, and 105–108. For Ramesses IX, see F. Guilmant, *Le tombeau de Ramsès IX*, MIFAO 15 (Cairo, 1907), plates 24, 28–33, and 49–60; the two large representations from section five in the sarcophagus chamber are on plates 89 and 91.

On the arrangement of the book and on the texts added on behalf of the king, see F. Abitz, *Pharao als Gott in den Unterweltsbüchern des Neuen Reiches*, OBO 146 (Freiburg and Göttingen, 1995), pp. 102–134. P. Barguet draws attention to parallels with the myth of Osiris, namely the reassembling of his dismembered body and his resurrection, in *RdE* 28 (1976): 25–37.

The Book of the Earth

The basic edition of the text, with a translation into French, remains that of A. Piankoff, *La création du disque solaire* (Cairo, 1953). The version of Ramesses VI was published by Piankoff, *The Tomb of Ramesses VI*, Bollingen Series 40/1 (New York, 1954), plates 111–121, 127–137, and 140, with an English translation on pp. 327–376; there are color reproductions in Hornung, *Tal der Könige: Die Ruhestätte der Pharaonen* (Mainz, 1990), pp. 133–134, 162, and 164. For Ramesses VII, see E. Hornung, *Zwei ramessidische Königsgräber: Ramses IV. und Ramses VII.* (Mainz, 1990), p. 88 and plates 116–119. The individual scenes employed by Sethos I and Osorkon II are published by H. Frankfort, *The Cenotaph of Seti I at Abydos*, MEES 39 (London, 1933), plate 87, and P. Montet, *Tanis: Douze années de fouilles dans une capitale oubliée du delta égyptien* (Paris, 1942), vol. 1, plate 37.

On the structure and content of the book, see W. Barta, *Die Bedeutung der Jenseitsbücher für den verstorbenen König*, MÄS 42 (Munich, 1985), pp. 65–67 and 123–128, and idem, *GM* 98 (1987): 7–9; on the content, see also B. H. Stricker, *De geboorte van Horus*, 5 vols. (Leiden, 1963–1989); on his "embryologic" explanation, cf. the comments by T. DuQuesne, *DE* 26 (1993): 97–105. Important observations on the structure and meaning of the book are found in F. Abitz, *Baugeschichte und Dekoration des Grabes Ramses' VI.*, OBO 89 (Freiburg and Göttingen, 1989), pp. 118–133, and idem, *Pharao als Gott in den Unterweltsbüchern des Neuen Reiches*, OBO 146 (Freiburg and Göttingen, 1995), pp. 135–173. There is a translation into German, though with the parts evidently in the wrong order, in Hornung, *Die Unterweltsbücher der Ägypter* (Zurich, 1992), pp. 425–480.

On the scene with Aker, see S. Schott, *Zum Weltbild der Jenseitsführer des Neuen Reiches*, NAWG 1965/11, pp. 188–190. An explanation of the scene with the birth of the stars as a water-clock was offered by P. Barguet, *RdE* 30 (1978): 51–56; see also W. Westendorf, *GM* 134 (1993): 102.

Miscellaneous Scenes

Ceiling of corridor F in the tomb of Ramesses VI: On the barque, see H. Grapow and H. Schäfer, *ZÄS* 73 (1937): 97–102, and the further remarks by Schäfer, *MDAIK* 8

(1939): 147–155, and Grapow, *ZÄS* 81 (1956): 24–28. The entire ceiling, along with the parallel in the tomb of Ramesses IX, is described by A. Piankoff and Ch. Maystre, *BIFAO* 38 (1939): 65–70, with plates V–VI; on the ceiling of Ramesses VI, see further Piankoff, *The Tomb of Ramesses VI*, Bollingen Series 40/1 (New York, 1954), pp. 433–434, with fig. 139 and plates 173–176 (F) and pp. 435–437, with plates 178–182 (G). On the ceiling of corridor F, see also F. Abitz, *Zur Baugeschichte und Dekoration des Grabes Ramses' VI.*, OBO 89 (Freiburg and Göttingen, 1989), pp. 144–150. An extract from the ceiling of the tomb of Ramesses IX, which is lacking in Guilmant's publication of the tomb, is given by J.-F. Champollion, *Monuments de l'Égypte et de la Nubie* (Paris, 1845), vol. 3, plate 270 = E. Hornung, *Tal der Könige: Ruhestätte der Pharaonen* (Mainz, 1990), p. 137 (ibid., p. 146: fig. 117 is not from the tomb of Ramesses IX, but from that of Ramesses VI).

Ceiling of corridor G in the tomb of Ramesses VI: The protective representation is treated by F. Abitz, *Zur Baugeschichte und Dekoration des Grabes Ramses' VI.*, OBO 89 (Freiburg and Göttingen, 1989) pp. 157–158 (and see ibid., pp. 150–154, on the ceiling of G generally), and, with its enigmatic captions, by E. Hornung, in J. H. Kamstra, H. Milde, and K. Wagtendonk, eds., *Funerary Symbols and Religion: Essays Dedicated to Professor M. S. H. G. Heerma van Voss on the Occasion of His Retirement from the Chair of the History of Ancient Religions at the University of Amsterdam* (Kampen, 1988), pp. 45–51. Improvements, along with a first treatment of the representations and texts in the decoration of the ceiling of G, are supplied by J. C. Darnell in "The Enigmatic Netherworld Books of the Solar-Osirian Unity" (Ph.D. diss., University of Chicago, 1995).

Ceiling of anteroom H in the tomb of Ramesses VI: The material is published by A. Piankoff, *The Tomb of Ramesses VI*, Bollingen Series 40/1 (New York, 1954), pp. 439–441, with fig. 142 and plates 183–185 (the ceiling of H) and plates 101–102 (the "protective representation"). On H, see also F. Abitz, *Zur Baugeschichte und Dekoration des Grabes Ramses' VI.*, OBO 89 (Freiburg and Göttingen, 1989), pp. 154–156.

Side walls of the sarcophagus chamber in the tomb of Ramesses VII: The material is published by A. Piankoff, *ASAE* 55 (1958): 150–155, with plates IV–IX, and E. Hornung, *Zwei ramessidische Königsgräber: Ramses IV. und Ramses VII.* (Mainz, 1990), pp. 63–71, with plates 11 and 116–119. On the scene with the crocodile, see E. Brunner–Traut in W. Helck, ed., *Festschrift für Siegfried Schott zu seinem 70. Geburtstag* (Wiesbaden, 1968), pp. 35–37. The parallel in the tomb of Ramses IX is represented by F. Guilmant, *Le tombeau de Ramsès IX*, MIFAO 15 (Cairo, 1907), plate 92, and Hornung, *Tal der Könige: Ruhestätte der Pharaonen* (Mainz, 1990), p. 116, fig. 88.

Right wall of the third corridor in the tomb of Ramesses IX: The entire wall is reproduced in facsimile by F. Guilmant, *Le tombeau de Ramsès IX*, MIFAO 15 (Cairo, 1907), plates 63 and 76–81. The figure of Osiris, with a parallel on a papyrus of Dynasty 21, was already treated by A. Piankoff, *ASAE* 49 (1949): 138–144, and on the entire wall, see E. Hornung, in J. Osing and G. Dreyer, eds., *Form und Mass: Beiträge zur Literatur, Sprache und Kunst des alten Ägypten, Festschrift für Gerhard Fecht zum 70. Geburtstag am 6. Februar 1987*, ÄAT 12 (Wiesbaden, 1987), pp. 226–237; F. Abitz, *SAK* 17 (1990): 25–28; and J. C. Darnell, "The Enigmatic Netherworld Books of the Solar-Osirian Unity" (Ph.D. diss., University of Chicago, 1995). For a color detail of the circles in the upper register, see E. Hornung, *Tal der Könige: Ruhestätte der Pharaonen* (Mainz, 1990), p. 148, fig. 126.

Sequence of scenes on sarcophagi: On the sarcophagus in Vienna and parallels, see E. von Bergmann, *RT* 6 (1885): 141–158. On the scene dealing with time, see K. Myśliwiec, in *Bulletin du Centenaire*, supplement to *BIFAO* 81 (Cairo, 1981), pp. 91–106; see also E. Hornung, *Zwei ramessidische Königsgräber: Ramses IV. und Ramses VII.* (Mainz, 1990), pp. 120–126, with plates 92–93.

The Books of the Sky

The Book of Nut

All the preserved texts are in O. Neugebauer and R. A. Parker, *Egyptian Astronomical Texts*, vol. 1, BES 3 (Providence, 1960), plates 44–51; the Demotic commentary is also reconsidered there. The latter was first published by H. O. Lange and O. Neugebauer, *Papyrus Carlsberg No. I. Ein hieratisch-demotischer kosmologischer Text*, DVS 1/2 (Copenhagen, 1940). There is also the complementary fragment from the burial chamber in the tomb of Mutirdis (TT 410), published by J. Assmann, *Das Grab der Mutirdis* (Mainz, 1977), pp. 85–88, with plate 39.

There is a translation into German and a commentary by E. Hornung, *Zwei ramessidische Königsgräber: Ramses IV. und Ramses VII.* (Mainz, 1990), pp. 92–96. On certain grammatical problems, see R. A. Parker, *RdE* 10 (1955): 49–59. On an astronomical explanation of the calendars of decans, see W. Barta, *SAK* 9 (1981): 85–103, and Ch. Leitz, *Studien zur ägyptischen Astronomie*, ÄgAbh 49, 2d ed. (1991), pp. 49–57. A detailed treatment of the book, with a translation and an astronomical commentary, has been offered by M. Clagett, *Ancient Egyptian Science*, vol. 2 (Philadelphia, 1995), pp. 357–403. See also J. P. Allen, *Genesis in Egypt: The Philosophy of Ancient Egyptian Creation Accounts*, YES 2 (New Haven, 1988), pp. 1–7.

The Book of the Day

The basic publications are by A. Piankoff, *Le Livre du jour et de la nuit*, BE 13 (Cairo, 1942), and idem, *ASAE* 41 (1941): 151–158 (tomb of Ramose); and P. Montet, *Tanis: Douze années de fouilles dans une capitale oubliée du delta égyptien*, vol. 1 (Paris, 1947), plate 25, and *Tanis*, vol. 3 (Paris, 1960), plates 29 and 31–32. Piankoff's edition offers a French translation, and an English translation appears in his *Tomb of Ramesses VI*, Bollingen Series 40/1 (New York, 1954), pp. 389–407; there is as yet no translation into German. The cryptographically written hymn of the Eastern Souls, along with parallels from Medinet Habu and the edifice of Taharqa at Karnak, have been treated by M. C. Betrò, *EVO* 12 (1989): 37–54, and the liturgical texts to the hours of the day by S. K. Doll, in W. K. Simpson and W. M. Davis, eds., *Studies in Ancient Egypt, the Aegean, and the Sudan: Essays in Honor of Dows Dunham on the Occasion of His 90th Birthday, June 1, 1980* (Boston, 1981), pp. 43–54, and idem, "Texts and Decoration on the Napatan Sarcophagi of Anlamani and Aspelta"(Ph.D. diss., Brandeis University, 1978). References to further sources on papyri are furnished by J. Osing, *Aspects de la culture pharaonique: Quatre leçons au Collège de France (février-mars 1989)*, MAIBL NS 12 (Paris, 1992), p. 43, and parallels to protective divine beings at Edfu are noted by J.-C. Goyon, *Les Dieux-gardiens et la genèse des temples d'après les textes égyptiens de l'époque gréco-romaine: Les soixante d'Edfou et les soixante-dix-sept dieux de*

Pharbaethos (Cairo, 1985), vol. 1, p. 130, n. 3. The texts of the hours at Edfu are to be found in E. Chassinat, *Le Temple d'Edfou*, vol. 3 (Cairo, 1928), pp. 213–229; see also J. Assmann, *Liturgische Lieder an den Sonnengott*, MÄS 19 (Berlin, 1969), pp. 113–164. On the hymns to the hours of the day, see also idem, *Ägyptische Hymnen und Gebete* (Zurich, 1975), no.1–12, and on the first two hours of the day, see D. Kurth, *Treffpunkt der Götter: Inschriften aus dem Tempel des Horus von Edfu* (Zurich, 1994), pp. 133–136.

A related text praising the king as someone who, in the company of the "Eastern Bas," knows the course of the sun and its *arcana*, has been treated by J. Assmann, *Der König als Sonnenpriester*, ADAIK 7 (Glückstadt, 1970), and many times since. It occurs already in temples of Dynasty 18 (Deir el-Bahari and Luxor) and again in the tomb of Petamenophis from Dynasty 26.

The Book of the Night

A. Piankoff supplies photographs from the sarcophagus chamber of Ramesses VI in *Le Livre du jour et de la nuit*, BE 13 (Cairo, 1942); there is a translation into English by the same scholar in *The Tomb of Ramesses VI*, Bollingen Series 40/1 (New York, 1954), pp. 409–428. The selections translated by C. Lalouette, *Textes sacrées et textes profanes* (Paris, 1984): pp. 155–158, correspond to Piankoff's plates V–VIII. E. Hornung comments on the second to the fourth hours in the tomb of Ramesses IV in *Zwei ramessidische Königsgräber: Ramses IV. und Ramses VII.* (Mainz, 1990), pp. 96–100; the text of the second hour and two further short samples can be found in idem, *Die Unterweltsbücher der Ägypter* (Zurich, 1992), pp. 489–493. For the versions from Tanis, see P. Montet, *Tanis: Douze années de fouilles dans une capitale oubliée du delta égyptien*, vol. 1 (Paris, 1947), plate 25, and vol. 3 (Paris, 1960), plates 29–32. The fragment from the tomb of Mutirdis (TT 410) has been published by J. Assmann, *Das Grab der Mutirdis* (Mainz, 1977), pp. 88–89, with plate 39. For the versions of the texts in the temples, see idem, *Ägyptische Hymnen und Gebete* (Zurich, 1975), no. 13 and 14 (the concluding text of the book); J. Karkowski, *ET* 9 (1976): 69–70 (Deir el–Bahari); A. Piankoff, *ASAE* 42 (1943): 351–353 (Medinet Habu, including the jackals designated as the "Western *bas*," now in Oriental Institute Epigraphic Survey, *Medinet Habu* VI. OIP 84 (Chicago, 1963), plate 422); and R. A. Parker, J. Leclant, and J.-Cl. Goyon, *The Edifice of Taharqa by the Sacred Lake of Karnak*, BES 8 (Providence, 1979), p. 41 with plate 19 (Karnak). On the late sarcophagi, see A. Piankoff, *ASAE* 40 (1940): 665–668. Finally, there is the edition by G. Roulin, *Le Livre de la Nuit: Une composition égyptienne de l'au-delà*, OBO 147 (Freiburg and Göttingen, 1996).

The Litany of Re

For R. Pococke's description of Ramesses IV's version, see *A Description of the East, and Some Other Countries* (London, 1743), p. 98. The first edition, based on the versions of Sethos I and Ramesses IV, with a translation into French, was published by E. Naville, *La Litanie du Soleil* (Leipzig, 1875); his translation of the text into English appeared in *Records of the Past*, vol. 8 (London, 1876), pp. 103–128. The edition now used is that of E. Hornung, *Das Buch der Anbetung des Re im Westen (Sonnenlitanei)*, vol. 1: *Text* (autographed by A. Brodbeck), AH 2 (Geneva, 1975), and vol. 2: *Überset-zung und Kommentar*, AH 3 (Geneva, 1976). On the textual tradition, see also W. Schenkel, *Das Stemma der altägyptischen Sonnenlitanei: Grundlegung der Textgeschichte nach der Methode der Textkritik*, GO 6 (Wiesbaden, 1978). A complete English transla-tion is furnished by A. Piankoff, *The Litany of Re*, Bollingen Series 40/4 (New York, 1964), pp. 22–43, and a detailed survey by W. J. de Jong, *De Ibis* 10 (1985): 2–20.

Photographs now exist of the earliest version, that of Useramun, in E. Dziobek, *Die Gräber des Vezirs User-Amun, Theben Nr. 61 und 131*, AVDAIK 84 (Mainz, 1994), pp. 42–47 with plates 9–16 and 28–35 (note that there is already a complete title in this version). Photographs of the version on the mummy shroud of Tuthmosis III (now in Cairo and Boston) and a portion of the version of Sethos I (the right wall of the first corridor) are published by Piankoff, *The Litany of Re*, and the mummy shroud again by I. Munro, *Die Totenbuch-Handschriften der 18. Dynastie im Ägyptis-chen Museum Cairo* (Wiesbaden, 1994). There is a complete publication of the ver-sion of Sethos I in H. Burton and E. Hornung, *The Tomb of Seti I/Das Grab Sethos' I.* (Zurich, 1991), plates 2–21 and 23–31, with the ceiling text on plate 42b; Belzoni's unpublished drawings, now in Bristol, permit some further restorations. The ver-sion of Ramesses II at Abydos was published, though the wrong way around, by A. Mariette, *Abydos*, vol. 2, plates 14–17; for some of the figures in the Osireion, see H. Frankfort, *The Cenotaph of Seti I at Abydos*, MEES 39, vol. 2, plates 71–72. For the beginning of Merneptah's version of the book, see E. Hornung, *Tal der Könige: Die Ruhestätte der Pharaonen* (Zurich, 1983), p. 111, fig. 77, and for further material from this tomb, see Piankoff, *The Litany of Re*, plates 8–9, and *ASAE* 6 (1905), plate IV after p. 192; a further fragment, discovered by J. Romer in the tomb of Ramesses XI, has not yet been published. The entire left wall from the version of Sethos II is given in Piankoff, *The Litany of Re*, plates 3–7, and the beginning of Siptah's version in Th. M. Davis, *The Tomb of Siphtah* (London, 1908). A fragment from the tomb of Sethos II in the British Museum (EA 1378) completes lines 229–232 (advisement from M. L. Bierbrier). All that is preserved of the version in the tomb of Ramesses IV is found in E. Hornung, *Zwei ramessidische Königsgräber: Ramses IV. und Ramses VII.* (Mainz, 1990), plates 18–25 and 31–41, and there is also a complete hand copy by Naville, *La Litanie du soleil*, plates 34–49; for Ramesses IX, there re-mains the edition of F. Guilmant, *Le Tombeau de Ramsès IX* (Cairo, 1907), plate 7 and 11–19, with the figures on plates 38–41.

A selection from the papyri is given in Piankoff, *The Litany of Re*, pp. 66–128. The two versions in temples of the Late Period are published in R. A. Parker, J. Leclant, and J.-Cl. Goyon, *The Edifice of Taharqa by the Sacred Lake of Karnak*, BES 8 (Provi-dence, 1979), pp. 30–35 with plates 12–15, and C. Traunecker, F. Le Saout, and O. Masson, *La Chapelle d'Achôris à Karnak* (Paris, 1981), pp. 55–60 with plate XII. The version in the tomb of Aba (TT 36) is published by K. P. Kuhlmann and W. Schenkel, *Das Grab des Ibi, Obergutsverwalters der Gottesgemahlin des Amun*, AVDAIK 15 (Mainz, 1983), vol. 1, pp. 254–256 with plates 146–147 and 150, while selections from the tomb of Mentuemhet are published by J. Leclant, *Montouemhat: Quatrième prophète d'Amon, prince de la ville*, BE 35 (Cairo, 1961), plate 60, and Pi-ankoff, *The Litany of Re*, plate 2; for the sarcophagus of Nectanebo II, see H. Jenni, *Das Dekorationsprogramm des Sarkophages Nektanebos' II*, AH 12 (Geneva, 1986).

The distribution of the text in the Ramesside royal tombs has been treated by W. Barta, *GM* 71 (1984): 7–10; he envisions a circular movement that comprehends the cyclical course of the sun, and he also stresses the special position of the ceiling text. On the Great Litany and its figures, see idem, *ZÄS* 113 (1986): 83–88, and on the concept *kheperu*, see idem, *ZÄS* 109 (1982): 81–86. The development of the figures of the *kheperu* of the sun god into independent deities is also treated by E. Hornung, in H.-J. Klimkeit, ed., *Götterbild in Kunst und Schrift* (Bonn, 1984), pp. 37–60. A brief introduction to the book, with a fresh translation of the title and the Great Litany, is offered by M. Clagett, *Ancient Egyptian Science: A Source Book*, vol. 1 (Philadelphia, 1989), pp. 511–529. On the appearance of portions of the litany in the Book of the Dead, see E. Hornung, in *Hommages à François Daumas* (Montpellier, 1986), pp. 427–428. On the structure and meaning of the book, see also F. Abitz, *Pharao als Gott in den Unterweltsbüchern des Neuen Reiches*, OBO 146 (Freiburg and Göttingen, 1995), pp. 51–72. The new explanation of the figure to the title is given by J. C. Darnell in "The Enigmatic Netherworld Books of the Solar-Osirian Unity" (Ph.D. diss. University of Chicago, 1995).

The Book of the Heavenly Cow

The first edition of the version in the tomb of Sethos I was published by E. Naville, *TSBA* 4 (1876): 1–19, and of the version in the tomb of Ramesses III by idem, *TSBA* 8 (1885): 412–420. Ch. Maystre's edition in *BIFAO* 40 (1941): 53–115 rested on a broader textual basis, though it contained no translation; Tutankhamun's version was subsequently published by A. Piankoff in *The Shrines of Tut-Ankh-Amon*, Bollingen Series 40/2 (New York, 1955), pp. 26–37 with fig. 47, and in *Les chapelles de Tout-Ankh-Amon*, MIFAO 72 (Cairo, 1952), pp. 17–18 and plate I. E. Hornung provides an improved text edition and discussion, *Der ägyptische Mythos von der Himmelskuh: Eine Ätiologie des Unvollkommenen*, 2d ed., OBO 46 (Freiburg and Göttingen, 1991). N. Giulhou published a further edition offering scarcely any advances in *Le Vieillesse des dieux* (Montpellier, 1989). A. Roccati makes reference to the papyrus in Turin in *BSFE* 99 (1984): 23 with n. 35. A further, incomplete (to verse 246) translation is offered by C. Lalouette, *Textes sacrés et textes profanes de l'ancienne Égypte*, vol. 2 (Paris, 1987), pp. 46–52. For the rest, most translations are restricted to the first part, which deals with the rebellion and punishment of humankind. On its inclusion in the Book of the Faiyum, see H. Beinlich, *Das Buch vom Fayum: Zum religiösen Eigenverständnis einer ägyptischen Landschaft*, ÄgAbh 51 (Wiesbaden, 1991), cols. 110–112 of the text.

The heavenly cow from Tutankhamun's shrine is represented in K. el-Mallakh and A. C. Brackman, *The Gold of Tutankhamen* (New York, 1978), plate 39, and see also Piankoff, *The Shrines of Tut-Ankh-Amon*, plate before p. 27. Besides the edition by Hornung, the color copy of the heavenly cow in the tomb of Sethos I by R. Hay also appears in E. Hornung, *Tal der Könige: Die Ruhestätte der Pharaonen* (Zurich, 1983), p. 176, fig. 149, and another old copy by H. Salt is found in the catalog of the exhibit *Sethos—ein Pharaonengrab* (Basel, 1991), p. 90; the present condition of Sethos's version can be seen in H. Burton and E. Hornung, *The Tomb of Pharaoh Seti I/Das Grab Sethos' I.* (Zurich, 1991), plates 154–159.

Additions to the bibliography in Hornung, *Mythos von der Himmelskuh*, pp. XI–XII: R. T. Rundle Clark, *Myth and Symbol in Ancient Egypt* (London, 1959), pp. 181–185 (translation through verse 163), and E. Bresciani, *Letteratura e poesia dell' antico Egitto* (Turin, 1969), pp. 227–229 (through verse 91). A partial English translation appears in M. Clagett, *Ancient Egyptian Science*, vol. 1 (Philadelphia, 1989), pp. 537–542. D. Lorton has commented on the date of the text in *BO* 40 (1983): 609–616, offering further arguments in favor of the Amarna Period. The meaning of the composition has been treated by H. Beinlich, *Das Buch vom Fayum*, pp. 316–317 and F. Abitz, *Pharao als Gott in den Unterweltsbüchern des Neuen Reiches*, OBO 146 (Freiburg and Göttingen, 1995), pp. 98–101.

The Book of Traversing Eternity

The long version was first published by B. H. Stricker, *De egyptische mysterien: Pap. Leiden T 32*, OMRO 31 (Leiden, 1950), pp. 45–63; OMRO 34 (Leiden, 1953), pp. 13–31; and OMRO 37 (Leiden, 1956), pp. 49–67. A first edition of the short version was published by E. von Bergmann, *Das Buch vom Durchwandeln der Ewigkeit* (Vienna, 1877), and it was later published again, together with the stela in the Vatican, by E. A. W. Budge, *The Chapters of Coming Forth by Day, or the Theban Recension of the Book of the Dead*, vol. 3 (London, 1910), pp. 150–160. All the textual material, with a translation into French and a thorough discussion, has now been published by F. R. Herbin, *L. Livre de parcourir l'éternité*, OLA 58 (Leuven, 1994), with a foreword by Jan Assmann, who had already treated the book in *LÄ* II, cols. 54–55.

INDEX